People go to church to worship and, as is often quipped, to be 'hatched, matched and dispatched'. Yet these quintessential rites have been adapted in all sorts of ways by parishioners and clergy up and down the country, while a great number of 'blessings' and other services that are quite specific to individual churches are performed annually. Collectively, they create a rich variety of traditions, many of which are only known about locally.

Some of these liturgical traditions have survived unbroken over many centuries, others have been revived after a break during the twentieth century – while yet more continue to be invented. Some of these more recent traditions – such as Harvest Festivals and Christingle – are now so ubiquitous that many churchgoers are unaware of a time when they were not part of the yearly cycle of customs.

By drawing together, for the first time, detailed information about these popular customs of the church, Mark Lewis hopes to stimulate further interest, research and recording of these remarkable events.

Chapter contents:

The shaping of the ritual year
The people of the Church: privilege and tradition
The church and churchyard: customs and superstitions
The commemorating Church
The Church in the community
Festivals and customs of the Church year
Birth: rites, customs and beliefs
Marriage: wedding customs and beliefs
Death: funeral customs and beliefs

Gazetteer of church customs through the calendar year

✠ Days and Rites ✠

Popular Customs of the Church

Mark Lewis

Heart of Albion

Days and Rites
Popular Customs of the Church

Mark Lewis

Cover: The Wilkes Walk, Leighton Buzzard, 2010,
by Terry Warburton

ISBN 978-1-905646-23-4

Published by

Heart of Albion
113 High Street
Avebury, Marlborough
Wiltshire, SN8 1RF

albion@indigogroup.co.uk

Visit our Web site: www.hoap.co.uk

Printed in England by Booksprint

Contents

Acknowledgements

Research for this book has been informed by many sources, past and present and many individuals have contributed invaluable information from personal knowledge and experience. Others have helped in various ways in the preparation of the text. I am especially grateful to my wife Nina for offering suggestions in the arrangement of the text at every stage which also benefited from her rigorous proof-reading of the final manuscript. My daughter Anna helped to ease the pressure of writing by helping to compile the bibliography and checking citations. Geoff Jones is also to be thanked for helpful comments on the introduction and first chapter.

I am also indebted to my brother-in-law, Jonathan Shiels who is Master of the Worshipful Company of Parish Clerks, for his perceptive comments and factual knowledge on the history and contemporary life of the Company. Dr Helen Frisby of the University of the West of England is to be thanked for providing invaluable specialist advice on the structure and content of the chapter on Funeral rites. David Bishop, the Rev Keith Hale, Rev Richard Simmons, Rev Canon David Truby and Rev Edward Ward for providing helpful advice on the history and contemporary status of 'church clypping' ceremonies in their respective parishes. I am very grateful to Averil Shepherd for helping out with imagery and also for her very informative website (www.calendarcustoms.com) which helped considerably in confirming the contemporary status of many local customs.

I also wish to express my gratitude to the following individuals who have contributed in various ways by advising on the history and status of particular customs, corroborating details or offering help in sourcing illustrations: Dr Margaret Bray, Rev Alison Clarke, Tony Fairclough, Rev Grant Fellows, Marika Footring, Dominic Harbour, Helen Gray, Rev Canon Paul Greenwell, Rev Peter Green, Paul Handley, Robert Hargreaves, Jeremy Harte, Rev Richard Holden, Mike Jones, Mike Lister, Iwan Llwyd, Rev Erwin Lammens, David Longford, Howard Martin, Kirsty McHugh, Victoria Neville, Benedict Parsons, Mike Paterson, Rev Hazel Robinson, Christopher Robinson, Doc Rowe, Rev John Twisleton, Dr Carole Ulanowsky-Rose, Terry Warburton MBE, David Wendon, Calvin Williams and Cressida Williams.

The Julian and Gregorian Calendars

Many celebratory customs associated with a particular festival do not necessarily occur on the same date. These anomalies were caused by changes to the calendar, imposed in the sixteenth century. Prior to this time, the Julian Calendar introduced by Julius Caesar in 45 BC was the system in general use throughout Western Europe. This arrangement was based on a solar year of 365¼ days and, to allow for the odd quarter of a day, every fourth year was ordained as a leap year containing 366 days. However, errors were made in its application and the solar year was too long by 11 minutes and 14 seconds. It was not until 1582 that the situation was corrected when Pope Gregory XIII harmonised the calendar by adding ten days so that 5 October became 15 October. This meant that the spring equinox which had fallen on 21 March in the Roman period, occurred on 11 March in 1582. Gregory's objective was also motivated by a desire to restore the position as it stood in AD 325 when he believed the Council of Nicea had laid down the rules for the calculation of Easter.

The change to the Gregorian calendar was soon adopted by most Catholic countries but Protestant Britain rejected this as popish nonsense and continued to use the Julian calendar until much later. The change was referred to as the 'New Style' and was finally adopted by England and Scotland in 1752 when Parliament decreed that 2 September should be immediately followed by 14 September. A further difficulty which had to be embraced was the traditional beginning of the civil or legal year in England which began on 25 March (Lady Day) while European countries followed the Gregorian system and started the year on 1 January. The calendar change was not well-received by many citizens and riots occurred in some areas with ignorant people believing they had been cheated. The popular cry of the time was: 'Give us back our eleven days!' Some communities remained loyal to the Julian calendar and the eleven-day variation caused events to acquire the prefix 'Old'. For example, in England, 12 May was often referred to as 'Old May Day'. A few events established within the old calendar still survive although the effect of subtle computational errors and a variety of other factors means that the difference does not always amount to eleven days. Many early books on folklore designate certain celebrations according to this system.

The Clowns' Service, Holy Trinity Church, Dalston, London.
Photograph by Doc Rowe.

Introduction

Religious practice was until recently at the centre of Western society. Every English parish owes its origin to the existence of a church building which in times past, was the focus of communal life. In the larger social picture, the Church of England is bound up with national and cultural identity and, in spite of the recent loss of influence, its traditions are still deeply interwoven with the communities it serves. Even a brief scrutiny of British calendar customs reveals a considerable number of events that continue to have strong associations with Church life.

The collective and social character of the Church has always expressed itself through a diversity of ritual practices and charitable acts. However, local communities have always made the Church their own by taking from it that which satisfies their individual or local needs. In addition to the weekly round of Sunday services and baptisms, weddings and funerals, the parish church has throughout its history, been the setting for numerous public activities. These rituals have been essential in developing fellowship and promoting social bonding, as well as addressing the practical challenge of raising parish funds. The historical record of the ecclesiastical year reveals a rich body of colourful customs and associated folklore. These have included holy day celebrations, ales, wakes, parish doles, perambulations, and localised commemorative events. Many communal traditions continue to the present day, sometimes in renewed or adapted forms, but in some measure they all function to unite sacred and secular life.

Church traditions were widely reported in the early literature of folklore but they became a mid-nineteenth century preoccupation when the widespread collecting of customs and superstitions was at its peak. The scope of the subject has proved to be enormous. It embraces a wealth of local legends, tales of ghosts, secret tunnels, unconventional clerics, folk cures and curious ecclesiastical artefacts. However, it was the calendar customs – seasonal rituals and popular superstitions at the heart of Church life – that seemed to provide the most compelling material for Victorian folklorists. Several volumes appeared from the 1850s onwards, documenting a range of beliefs and practices clustered around the life of the official Church, while also revealing a body of custom and superstition that would be more accurately described as 'folk Christianity'. Many authors of these books were clergymen. J.C. Atkinson, Sabine Baring-Gould, T.F. Thistelton Dyer, George Tyack and Edward Vaux are some of the prominent clerical names and typical of their time. They were not just men in holy orders, but scholarly antiquarians, archaeologists and ecclesiologists, caught up in the growing interest in folklore. The work of these writers provides some of the richest material and is still a valued resource for contemporary Church folklorists. This book draws significantly on their findings.

It is typical of Victorian ecclesiastical collectors of folklore that little attempt was made to explain or interpret the origins of some of the more obscure findings, especially where local meanings had long since been lost. They were writing in an intellectual climate of armchair scholarship which promoted 'survivalism', the view that sees folklore as the vestigial remains of a more primitive world. However, it has to be affirmed that ecclesiastical traditions, by their very nature, are supported by some well-attested biblical and liturgical practices that consolidated in the developing early Church. Even so, there has always been a dichotomy in British religious life and ritual observance. History reveals that after the first arrival of Christianity in pagan Britain during the fourth century, religious practice became embedded in two forms of expression; these may broadly be defined as 'official' and 'popular religion'. While the former stressed a devotional life focussed on established doctrine, its popular counterpart was a loose medley of pagan superstition practised under a thin veneer of Christian belief. Mainstream clerical Christianity was regarded by ordinary parishioners as pessimistic, too vague in its assurances and oriented too much towards future salvation. Popular Christianity was by contrast, viewed as immediate, pragmatic and optimistic; its pagan trappings and unorthodox conceptions enriched the prevailing culture of folk medicine and offered an accessible and tangible means of coping with the everyday trials of human existence. Despite vigorous reforms to purge religion of superstitious practices, both forms coexisted, usually in tension with each other, but sometimes in harmony, until comparatively recent times.

The relationship between these two religious forms is a theme that permeates this book. The intention is to shed light on the history and current status of the many national and local customs beyond regular Sunday ritual observances. Beginning with an historical overview of the developments that lead to the ecclesiastical year as it is known today, the traditions associated with clergy and laity, church buildings, churchyards and ecclesiastical artefacts are explored. Subsequent chapters investigate the special commemorative services, pilgrimages, processions, public blessings, wakes and feasts and the primary festivals of the Church year. The last chapters examine the customs and folklore associated with the life-cycle rituals such as baptism, confirmation, marriage, churching and funerals.

This book then, is a 'warts and all' perspective with no particular theological or spiritual position. Nonetheless, it does not shy away from recounting the far-reaching pagan and superstitious legacy of the church. The tone of the book is not critical but is intended to be a celebration of Anglican Christianity and its people, festivals, ritual customs and folklore, old and new. While some of these traditions are observed nationally around the major festivals of the church year, others are little known and unique to specific localities. A few practices, such as bequests and commemorative customs, border on the eccentric and to many readers they will seem quaint and arcane. Other customs are deeply moving and poetic in character. However, they are all part of a vigorous living tradition and have become inextricably woven into local community life, reassuringly helping to connect the past with the present. They draw in the faithful and those of no faith at all and still attract high levels of public interest and media coverage. Hopefully this book will arouse curiosity and stimulate further enquiry into important and sometimes frequently overlooked dimensions of Christian history and culture.

Religiosity is of course expressed in the contemporary world in an increasingly wide range of identities, values and belongings which are continually changing. However, custom has played, and still plays an important role in the life and work of the Church and continues to address the private spiritual needs of families and individuals. People still feel a need to sacralise the rites of passage; the religious commitment may sometimes be tenuous, but Christian baptisms, weddings and funerals have continuing value in the present because in a largely secular world that plays down the validity of sacred rituals, there is still a deep yearning to celebrate inner meanings with outward visible forms.

The rich legacy of custom and folklore associated with churches and cathedrals suggests that the essence of Christianity expressed through Church life has always been about relationship and attempting to bond community. The inherited traditions are even now, embedded in secular institutions but demonstrate a remarkable vitality and extraordinary capacity to resist change. The Christian tradition still has strong resonances in the twenty-first century and even among the contemporary die-hard secularists, there are some who willingly declare they are 'cultural' or 'tribal' Anglicans with an almost sentimental loyalty to Church tradition. There is certainly an innate conservatism in our religious culture and it may well be this dogged conformist streak that will ultimately ensure the survival of our most treasured Church customs and traditions.

Chapter One

The shaping of the ritual year

The spirit and character of the various Christian denominations in Britain have been shaped by many factors. But to understand how the folklore and customs associated with individual churches and chapels have evolved, we must turn back to the arrival of Christianity in pagan England. Much of our early understanding of this convergence of belief systems has traditionally focused on a letter from Pope Gregory the First in 601, which advised Archbishop Mellitus of Canterbury not to rush his English converts into new customs (Bede 1907: 45). Anglo-Saxons were to be baptised gradually so that their hold on pagan deities would be broken by degrees. Their annual festivities could be appropriated for Christian use. The old shrines were to be retained at least in the short term, and blessed with holy water. Only the idols were to be destroyed and replaced with Christian altars and relics. It was a simple and effective psychology; pagans would feel less threatened if their conversion took place within the established pattern of festivals and in the sacred spaces that were familiar to them. Gregory clearly displayed a sensitive understanding of the dynamics of religious conversion, but he was not unduly concerned about the collision of beliefs and practices that was taking place in the minds of the new converts. The result was a hybrid that according to Aaron Gurevich, perpetuated an 'ambivalent and grotesque world-view' (Gurevich 1988: 62) and a culture that owed little to official Church doctrine.

The emergence of 'popular Christianity'

So what did the pagans believe? The Christian world of sixth century Britain as much as the heathen world it had entered was populated by a vast array of spiritual beings. Even under the impact of a new and developing culture of faith, ordinary people believed they shared their lives with fiends, elves and dragons that were not just commonplace in legend but actively interfered with the processes of daily life. Animism was the prevailing spiritual underpinning of the profane world. There was a force or some kind of life-principle in all things, both animate and inanimate and there was a mutual influence among things. Indeed, there was no clear separation between the spiritual and physical worlds.

There were always apparent contradictions between the pagan and Christian worldviews. Paganism was after all, a diverse and pluralistic group of cults and observances without any clear unifying principle, compared to the cohesive monotheistic Christian cosmos which is intended to be contemplated and worshipped. By contrast, paganism was a resource that could be used and applied to tangible life situations as the need demanded (Obelkevich 1976: 281). In reality, this meant that supernatural enchantment pervaded the entire world of the common people, their everyday habits, beliefs and behaviour. Magic had always been a necessary weapon against the destructive power of the natural world. The fifth to eighth century was a particularly troubled period throughout Europe, characterised by frequent bad harvests and consequent periods of famine, high mortality, civil wars and regular conflicts with invading hostile groups. Epidemics and virulent infections were commonplace and other natural catastrophes, including earthquakes, were a frightening reality. There was also violent oppression of the common people by the ruling classes of the day. People lived in a continual state of poverty and insecurity so it is not surprising that the immediacy and variety of pagan practices held such a wide appeal. The holy was not conceived as a distant remote world, but intimately bound up with the world here and now. R.A. Markus observed:

> The divine was always there like a huge electric charge
> waiting to break through the cloud, to be earthed like the
> churches' lightning conductors – worship and the means
> provided for carrying it on: the altar, the church building,
> the community or one or other of its members.

(Markus 1990: 23)

However, there has always been a danger of over-emphasising the perceived pre-Christian influences on the developing English Church. Magic has all too frequently been assumed to be synonymous with religious practice. Karen Jolly (1996) has explored the Christian culture of the eighth to tenth centuries and drawn a distinction between magic in its traditional understanding of sorcery and the character of formal religious practice. She observes that magical practice was not itself born out of Christian belief but observed by people who still considered themselves to be fully Christian in belief and identity. Pagan beliefs were not entirely eclipsed by Christianity but were gradually assimilated or transformed by it. Jolly observes that:

> Anglo-Saxon Christians were not suffering from a split personality; rather they created a wholeness out of their mixed heritages.

(Jolly 1996: 11).

The blending of Christian liturgy and indigenous Germanic customs gave birth to 'popular' or 'folk Christianity', which is significantly different from its 'official' counterpart. It would probably not have been understood by its practitioners as developing from the authorised Christian Church. Medieval popular belief however, cannot easily be understood in clear-cut 'dualist' terms as many modern theorists have tended to imply. While religious thinking is often discussed in terms of the doctrines of formal religion, in reality the historical record suggests that most Christians were clearly more secure with a wider range of beliefs (Trubshaw 2002: 42). 'Popular Christianity' has been integral to religious practice until comparatively recent times although vestigial elements still remain in contemporary culture.

The power of the clergy

The clergy as the authorised representatives of the established Church were paradoxically central to the development of popular belief; all kinds of special powers and virtues were attributed to them. The earliest priests were men of basic education and often recruited from the rural communities in which they served (Watkins 2004: 141–2). However, as medieval university education developed, priests emerged as learned men who were usually the most literate and well-informed members of their parish. The clergy were defined by their role as mediators of the religious power of the Church and generally regarded with a measure of awe. They presided over powerful rituals and were further set apart in the community by their celibate status. For Medieval Christians there was little distinction to make between the priestly vocation of a clergyman and that of a magician. Sorcerers, cunning men and astrologers were active in many communities and the parish priest was generally viewed in rural areas as simply another member of the magical fraternity.

The mere touch of a priest was credited with bringing about healing and he represented an institution which has been aptly described by Alan Smith as 'a psychic powerhouse and often indeed a veritable pharmacopoeia' (Smith 1971: 19). In popular belief the rituals of the Church were viewed as potent sources of remedial and protective magic. The Mass was the central rite and deemed to be an especially magical event by virtue of the consecration of bread and wine, transforming them into the body and blood of Jesus Christ. The consecrated Eucharistic host was particularly valued for its amuletic properties (Wilson 2004: 461). Holy water was equally potent because of its ceremonial blessing at the hands of the clergy and was in demand for repelling demons, curing the sick and protecting houses. The rituals surrounding baptism, marriage and death also had a magical element and through performing these rites, a priest could ensure the fertility of the fields, secure physical wellbeing and guarantee healthy livestock.

Because the sanctuary of the church was the ritual domain of the clergy, all kinds of images, amulets and objects placed near the altar could be imbued with special significance and take on magical powers during the celebration of the mass. The clergy often spoke out against such superstitious practices. Even so, they sometimes abused their position and colluded with the culture of superstition. There was a modest level of acceptance of magical attitudes, especially towards the blessed sacrament, which no doubt ensured sizeable congregations. Some priests certainly had direct involvement with magical rites if only for their own protection. For example, even as late as the early eighteenth century, a Norfolk vicar was recorded as carrying a written charm for ague upon his person (Dawson 1932).

Nevertheless, supernatural power of divine origin did not just reside with the clergy. The reigning monarch possessed the 'Divine Right of Kings' and was also deemed to be a powerful mediator between humanity and God. Monarchs demonstrated their particular divine calling on Good Friday at the Chapel Royal, where silver rings were blessed in a special ceremony and were believed to protect against cramps and epilepsy. The origin is credited to Edward II but the custom was developed by Edward III in the belief that the touch of the monarch would have healing power (Crawfurd 1917). So superstition concerning the mediation of divine power to secure specific human needs was rife at every level of the social hierarchy.

Superstition and religion

What actually constitutes superstition? When religious believers denounce religious practice as inferior or critique their fellow believers for practising their faith 'incorrectly' they invariably dismiss it as 'superstitious'. There is no consensus among folklorists and anthropologists on the meaning of the word. Throughout the history of Western Christianity the faithful have continually appropriated new arguments for designating correct and true beliefs and every shift in Christian thought from the Renaissance to the Enlightenment has added new dimensions to the debate. However, clearly the last word on superstition always resided with the Church!

In medieval Europe superstition meant a 'perversion of religion' and the theologians of the time laid down their own clear distinctions between religious and superstitious practice. The use of a consecrated object, for example, for any reason other than its designated purpose was considered 'superstitious'. Moreover, any attempt to manipulate natural events or attribute powers to objects in order to achieve personal gain, was deemed to be superstitious if it did not have the authorisation of the Church (Thomas 1997: 48). In its widest application, superstition has always been viewed by the official church as a deviation from religious orthodoxy or the attribution of importance to magical practices that affect or contradict the worship of the true God. Indeed, for the Protestant Reformers, anything that was contrary to that which had been ordained by God was unquestionably superstitious. As we will see throughout this book, any artefact or substance taken from consecrated ground was believed without question to be imbued with magical properties. These objects were superstitiously valued as protective amulets and everything from coffin nails to church bells could be revered as 'quasi-relics' (Wilson 2004: 465). The growing fear of witchcraft in the medieval period and the neurotic concerns it engendered in the populace also added considerably to a continuing culture of superstition.

The developing church year

Within this milieu of interwoven magic and religious practice, the early medieval Church worked out its mission, theology and community life. By the eleventh century monastic communities were thriving, the parish system was in place and church buildings had become feasts of colour, packed with imagery for biblical teaching. The Church at this time was highly mystical in its outlook and visible manifestations of faith were to be found everywhere. Spectacle was the order of the day and processions, mystery plays and other forms of drama were assimilated into the liturgy, especially around the great feasts. For the people of the medieval period, this mode of Christian practice was highly appropriate to support the illiteracy of those in rural communities. It was a proactive religion characterised by frequent encounter with ritual. Christina Larner confirms this:

> Religion was about doing things. It was about observance. It was about attending mass, giving money to the church, genuflection, going on pilgrimage. Such performances could complement rather than compete with magical animist beliefs and practices.

(Larner 1984: 118)

The ritual life of the Church quickly evolved into a distinctive structure. A linear pattern of religious activity began to emerge in the fourth century which, in its most developed form, we have inherited today. The earliest medieval calendar was characterised by a combination of celestial, pagan and ecclesiastical elements. An annual cycle of birth, death and rebirth were played out with the seasons, following the rise and fall of the sun through the solstice and the equinox. The agricultural year took centre stage because it was essential for human flourishing and survival. Its seasons have always been reflected in a busy round of economic activities and ritual action. The Celtic calendar, which was divided into four seasons and based on the farming cycle, had a profound influence on this.

As the ecclesiastical year shaped up around this natural calendar, the unfolding story of Jesus Christ told in the Gospels was narrated in an annual cycle, beginning at Advent and embracing Christmas, Epiphany, Lent, Easter and Ascension. The whole Christian narrative of birth, death and resurrection was easily grafted on to the older cycle of the solar year. Quarterly 'ember days' were also introduced and decreed as special times of prayer and fasting. Certainly some elements of the Church year barely concealed pre-Christian observances. For example, two high-profile pagan festivals, May Day and Midsummer's Day were named the feasts of St Philip and St John respectively. The seasonal festivals became the primary form of ritual observance and Sunday services were offered on a regular basis, although prior to the Reformation there was no law making it mandatory to attend them (Hutton 2011: 243).

The cult of the saints

The greatest impact on the liturgical year was the rapidly developing cult of the saints. Some were contemporaries of Jesus Christ, while others were extraordinary men and women whose proven Christian witness and suffering had earned them sanctification, canonisation and perpetual memory by the Church. Many saints' lives are obscure and lack any sound documentary evidence, which means that it is often difficult to separate fact from legend, but their attraction was undeniable and pilgrimages to the shrines of saints by those in search of healing miracles were undertaken on an astonishing scale. Votive offerings were placed by their tombs, which typically included candles, wax effigies, coins and jewellery – and even live offerings in the form of birds were not unknown. Objects such as crutches, which had been associated with apparently miraculous healings were also common (Finucane 1977: 96).

The popularity of the saints became a devotional phenomenon of Christian history and reached its peak in the fifteenth and sixteenth centuries. Imagery of the saints could be found everywhere: on cups and bowls, carved on lintels and emblazoned in stained glass windows. A statue of the patronal saint of a parish sometimes appeared in a niche in the church porch, representative of the dedication and probably also serving to enhance parochial identity (Marks 2004: 82–5). The names of saints were popularly given to children at baptism and by the fifteenth century they were being commonly bestowed on ships to protect them from storms and wreck (Wilson 2004: 80). Such was the enthusiasm for the saints in life that many parishioners wished to venerate their images in death. Bequests were frequently left in wills to honour them on masses, communion or with a devotional display of lights (Dendy 1959: 114; Duffy 1992: 157).

In general terms, the saints were soul-friends who could be called upon for protection and spiritual help in all manner of human affairs. Many were celebrated throughout the country and by the late medieval period, some took on a more 'specialist' mantle. Individual saints became the spiritual protectors for specific trades and crafts or were credited with healing particular diseases and afflictions. The feast of St Blaise (3 February), for example, was traditionally celebrated by workers in the woollen industry with colourful processions (Hole 1942: 33), but the saint could also be invoked for curing diseases of the throat. The reputation of the saints for effecting healing miracles owed much to their accessibility and the geographical location of their relics. Gurevich observed that the saints' role:

> found a much easier path to the consciousness of the
> common people than did the idea of a distant, invisible and
> awe-inspiring God. Attitudes towards God lacked the
> 'intimacy' and 'sincerity which united the faithful with the
> local saints

(Gurevich 1988: 43).

The early Church was steeped in notions of the miraculous and Christian leaders such as St Augustine were cautious about emphasising visible wonders. However for many believers, faith in the power of saintly bones became the very essence of medieval Christianity. In spite of early legislation prohibiting the removal and dismemberment of the dead, the escalating desire for holy relics became a widespread industry, particularly among the monastic orders, with easy opportunities for fraud. The remains of saints were taken around like a travelling theatre and the supernatural power of these sacred objects quickly dominated the landscape of Christianity across Europe. Ronald Finucane has noted that it was as if these venerated relics:

> emitted a kind of holy radioactivity that bombarded
> everything in the area and as early as the sixth century it
> was believed that objects placed next to them would absorb

some of their power and grow heavier. They affected oil in the lamps that burned above them, cloths placed nearby, water or wine which washed them, dust which settled on them, fragments of the tombs which enclosed them, gems or rings which touched them…

(Finucane 1977: 26)

The many magical springs to be found scattered around the country came to be designated as 'holy wells' and associated with individual saints, while still retaining their magical healing properties. The clergy soon recognised that the saints and their relics had powerful missionary advantages. To illiterate and uneducated rural congregations who were incapable of grasping even the most basic theological principles, the performance of miracles became a simple method of communicating the fundamental truth of Christianity (Finucane 1977: 21). The efficacy of saintly relics was deeply exaggerated by the clergy and they eventually acquired a meaning and importance far beyond anything originally intended by missionaries.

The saints' days

Saints' days became pivotal to the patterns of sacred and secular life. Devotional propriety required that over fifty days in the year were to be set apart from Sundays and solemnly dedicated to the saints. As the number of recognised saints increased during the first half of the middle ages, every day of the year could boast at least one saint who was commemorated on that date. There were also some regional differences in the calendar of the saints. Almost inevitably, the ecclesiastical year became burdened with saints' days resulting in an overcrowded calendar. Interestingly, even up until 1830 the Bank of England still closed on forty saints' days during the year; many of these were eventually dropped and replaced with national paid holidays.

All work, except that considered most essential to agricultural life, was forbidden. The faithful were expected to fast on the eve of the saint's day and to attend Mass and evensong on the day. By the later medieval period, the saints had become embedded in the popular memory. However, the emphasis had already begun to shift from devotion to the pragmatic exploitation of their celebrated days as useful markers for traditional farming practices, wakes, fairs and markets. These days were also opportunities for feasting and celebration but conversely they were viewed as times for idleness and unruly behaviour. As their religious meaning was gradually lost, they also became a focus for love divinations (Duffy 1992:13). By the seventeenth century the observance of saints' days was diminishing significantly as parishioners ignored all but the most popular feasts.

Curious calendar survivals, parodies and subversions

Inevitably there were a few localised customs in the church calendar that were zealously maintained by unquestioning parishioners. Many of these customs do not easily equate with the rhythmic developments of the church year and they still defy a satisfactory historical explanation. Balaams Ass Sunday, for example, was observed at Randwick and Hawkesbury in Gloucestershire up to the eighteenth century. On the second Sunday after Easter the story of Balaam (Numbers 22–24) was read and crowds of people gathered to hear the reading. It has been conjectured that this may have been a remnant from the days when miracle plays were performed (*Notes and Queries* [1889] 4: 178–9).

The Palm Sunday custom known as the 'Gad-whip ceremony' which took place at Caistor in Lincolnshire is also a great curiosity of church folklore. Every year a man, representing the proprietor of the nearby Broughton estate, came into Caistor church porch while the first lesson was being read and cracked a 'Gad-whip' three times. He then entered the church, and during the reading of the second lesson he approached the clergyman, holding the whip upright to which was tied a bag containing thirty pieces of silver. He knelt before the clergyman, and waved the whip three times round his head, and left the church at the end of the lesson (Brand 1813: 130–1). The origins of the custom do not seem to have been recorded although it is widely considered to have been some kind of condition of tenure. The ceremony was strongly denounced in the Houses of Parliament as irreverent and was last performed around 1850 (Roud 2006:127–8).

Other eccentricities were characterised by a conscious element of misrule such as 'Crack-Nut Sunday', observed at the parish church of Kingston-upon-Thames in Surrey until the early nineteenth century. Adults and children cracked nuts during the service on the Sunday before the eve of St Michael's Day (29 September). The intention seems to have been entirely disruptive and it was stated that the sound of cracking was so loud that the minister had to postpone his reading until silence was obtained! It was believed to have had some connection with the choosing of the bailiffs and other members of the corporate body at Michaelmas and may have also have occurred in other parishes (Brayley 1850 Vol 3: 41–42). Other annual customs had an equally seditious flavour with little connection to the devotional life of the church. Pelting the parson, hassock-throwing and pew-flapping are just some of the more subversive seasonal customs that do not always yield convincing explanations (see Chapters 2 and 3).

Christmas time also saw the election of a Lord of Misrule and boisterous wakes evolved at various other high points in the ecclesiastical calendar. The tradition upheld in many churches of enthroning a Boy Bishop on St Nicholas' Day (6 December) was seen as both parody and subversion (see Chapter 2) and often led to disorderly behaviour. Some of these customs might have been associated with 'lawless days' which prevailed in some localities, where established laws were briefly suspended and people could behave as they wished without fear of reprisals. Certain days in the calendar had only a tenuous religious significance, such as the Monday and Tuesday after the second week of Easter. These two days were known as Hocktide and groups of young men and women playfully held members of the opposite sex as hostages and only releasing them upon payment of a modest fine. The churchwardens collected this 'hock money' to help increase the parish funds (Cox 1913: 261–2), which had no doubt been depleted over the Easter period.

The impact of the Reformation

The greatest body blow to the worshipping life of the Church came with the sweeping reforms of Henry VIII. Before the beginning of the sixteenth century it was considered that the church was riddled with ignorance and idolatry. Priests fraudulently took money from the people to buy them out of purgatory and ensure their salvation. Corruption and immorality was endemic among the priesthood and as a consequence, anti-clericalism was soon rife among the laity. There was now a ruthless determination to stamp out 'popish' superstition in the life and ritual of the Church. So began a steady and protracted weakening of the medieval Church in favour of a strong culture of restructured Protestant churchmanship. Henry's changes to traditional religious practice were radical and decisive. Royal injunctions issued in 1538, declared that images and statues of saints were superstitious and to be destroyed; any surviving representations of saints were to be regarded only as memorials (Hutton 1994: 74–5). Miracles, pilgrimages and holy wells were forcefully denounced. Shrines to the saints were smashed and their relics were ridiculed as worthless. Most candles and lamps, especially those placed before the images of saints, were removed from churches. By the end of the English Reformation, chantry chapels had been demolished, church altars stripped and communion plate removed. Indeed, anything which smacked of 'popery' was routed out and condemned. Churches consequently became plain and bare with the intention of encouraging a more pure and direct communion with the unseen God. The material world as a domain of sacred experience was censured and instead, the reformers emphasised the development of the heart and mind of the believer. Outward ritual was to be replaced with the inner contemplation of biblical texts. Worship was directed towards preaching, and by the eighteenth century, sermons were stressing moral duty grounded in the inherent historical truths of the Bible.

The Reformation was driven by much more than an overhaul of scriptural values. The doctrinal disputes between Rome and Canterbury were not just a conflict between superstition and godliness but also reflected a tension between social order and the disorder that popular festivities were inclined to encourage. Even throughout the early medieval period, there had been various statutes proscribing dancing, feastings and games, especially during service time. Well into the Elizabethan period and beyond the continual suppression of holy days and their customs, such as wakes and church ales, was more concerned with licentiousness and social unrest than the finer points of religious belief and practice. Ronald Hutton has observed that the general distaste for festivities within the church was driven by two enduring themes within medieval Christian teaching:

> Disorder must be abhorrent to the 'divine magistrate' as to
> the human one and that merry-making are sins of the flesh.

(Hutton 1994: 71)

Holy days were the great offenders and deemed to be too abundant. They upset working patterns and productivity in favour of idleness and debauchery, especially in rural communities. There were sustained campaigns for their suppression and the more extreme reformers sought the complete abolition of saints' days which were regarded as major distractions from Sunday observance.

The Book of Common Prayer and the rise of the Puritans

The appearance of the Book of Common Prayer was the key moment in the Henrician reforms. This was destined to reshape the whole of the ecclesiastical calendar. Prior to its publication, most forms of parish worship in late medieval English churches followed the Latin Roman Rite, although there was considerable variation in regional practice which was generally termed 'local use'. The Use of Sarum which was established by St Osmund at Salisbury in the eleventh century became the commonest rite for ordering public worship, particularly in governing the Mass celebrated on Sundays and the great feast days.

The Book of Common Prayer was introduced in 1549 by Archbishop Cranmer and significantly influenced by the Sarum Use. A more reformed revision appeared in 1552 and this was the first prayer book to include the complete forms of service for daily and Sunday worship in English. The turbulent events which led to the English Civil War (1642–51) prompted another major revision in 1662 and this version is still used today in many parishes. The Prayer Book came to be regarded as a national devotional framework for the passage of the seasons, firmly centred on celebrating the life of Christ. It had a legitimising effect on the Church year although a major feature of the reformed ecclesiastical calendar was inevitably a severe reduction in the number of holy days.

A remodelled Church calendar was now firmly in place, but the Puritan movement which began during the reign of Elizabeth I (1558–1603) had a further deadening impact on the popular festivals during the year. The strict Puritan adherence to moral codes, closely following New Testament scriptures, had little place for joyful festivity. Church attendance became compulsory and worship was a simple affair with an even greater emphasis on moralistic preaching.

The Puritans also took great exception to minor aspects of church ceremonial. For example, the wearing of a surplice, the giving of a ring in marriage and the use of the sign of the cross were all condemned. Their objection to these ritual elements was based on the fact that there was no biblical authority to support them. The greatest casualties under the Puritan regime were Christmas, Easter and Whitsun, which were abolished in England in 1647 and ordered to be a time of fasting. There were many vocal protests and illegal attempts on the part of certain priests to hold services around these festivals, and they were only restored under Charles II in 1660.

The post-reformation church and ritual practice

By the end of the Middle Ages the festivities and pageantry which structured the year provided effective rituals for marking changes to the seasons, working patterns and community politics, while also helping to ease and shape transitions (Phythian-Adams 1972). However, while many of the annual customs may have been officially abolished during the Reformation, it was not so easy to eradicate them from the popular mind. Even during the Elizabethan period, many pre-Reformation church practices were to be found in a modified form. This 'calendrical consciousness' (Cressy 1989: 13) was still embedded in the lives of the people and the most important rituals of the church year were gradually transmuted into folk customs even after they had been driven out of formal religion (Hutton 1995: 113). The custom of 'palming' on Palm Sunday and the consumption of 'hot cross buns' on Good Friday are examples that typically do not seem to have attracted any vocal calls for reform. The saints' days had also been dramatically reduced as devotional observances, but some days such as All Souls, St Andrew and St Thomas, were appropriated as effective opportunities for the poor to solicit doles of money, food and drink within the parish (Bushaway 1982: 182).

During the late eighteenth and early nineteenth century, popular religion continued unabated, but became sufficiently disparate and localised to the extent that that certain activities did not significantly draw attention to themselves. 'Wise men' who offered charms and spells combining Biblical and astrological elements, persisted in rural parishes to a surprising degree with notable strongholds in Lancashire and Yorkshire (Rushton 1980). The belief in the power of exorcism still flourished in the West Country in particular, and certain local clergy were in demand as 'magician-parsons' (Brown 1961: 390). William Henderson attempted to explain this continuing attachment to popular Christianity by suggesting that earlier efforts to eradicate the cult of saints had probably served all too easily to direct the minds of the people to a 'supernatural system of another order' (Henderson 1879: 7).

The legacy of the Victorian church

By the mid-nineteenth century, the 'official' church witnessed a period of strong growth characterised by considerable energy and expansion. The founding of the Anglo-Catholic Oxford Movement in the 1830s fostered the reintroduction of various pre-reformation liturgical practices and the 1850s saw a growing preoccupation with high ritual throughout the Church of England. This culture of ritualism was strongly resisted in many quarters and it was seen by many as the return of papal superstition. Some of these ceremonies even landed participating clergy in courts and there was at least one imprisonment. Non-conformist churches were also spreading with equivalent fervour, but it was the rise of Methodism that was to become a profoundly important development; its ministry to rural areas found great popularity with the labouring classes. The Methodist Church preferred to ignore the practices of folk religion, but perhaps unwittingly encouraged them. At the beginning of the nineteenth century Wesleyan Methodists were openly expressing their belief in the reality of witchcraft and demonic possession. They also fiercely proclaimed divine intervention and retribution. Anglican clergy, not surprisingly, considered that these entrenched positions only served to further propagate superstitious beliefs among the masses (Davies 1997). In spite of this, Methodism flourished and became a forceful challenge to the Church of England in agricultural communities.

Popular customs associated with the church calendar began to disappear, influenced by the Victorian desire for moral improvement in all things. Some local customs were eradicated by the intervention of strong-willed and disapproving clergymen. Many of the charitable doles which had reached large numbers by the end of the eighteenth century were abandoned, either because they were no longer financially viable or because their origins were challenged and legitimate documentary evidence could not be found to support them. Other customs were transformed rather than abolished. So, for example, the Whitsuntide wakes and church ales which had attracted so much shameless revelry and rough sports were gradually tamed and developed into sober club walks and parades (Bushaway 1982: 253, 257) which generally ended with a decorous church service. While clerical ecclesiologists were cautiously lamenting the persistence of popular customs in many rural areas and dismissing them as superstitious 'pagan survivals' some new observances in mainstream church life were in the ascendant. The Victorians can take credit for bringing fresh additions to the ecclesiastical calendar of which the Harvest Festival is the probably most enduring example (see Chapter 6). This event was also carefully fostered as a more respectable replacement for the old established, disorderly celebrations that formally prevailed at the end of the harvest season. Several pre-Reformation practices such as sea, river and fishery blessings were also enthusiastically revived, and still remain popular in many parts of the country to this day.

Church customs and the twenty-first century challenge

Many customs that centred on ecclesiastical life were revived, remodelled or given a new lease of life in the early twentieth century. Controlled revivals of customs, such as beating of the bounds, well-dressings, church clypping and rush-bearings continue to be enthusiastically supported by various church communities. The four-hundred year-old cradle rocking ceremony held at Candlemas, which was revived at Blidworth in Nottinghamshire in 1922 is a robust example of an early custom that has once again become embedded in the local church calendar and proudly upheld by the community (see Chapter 6). The more colourful Church customs still maintain a hold on the public imagination and have become part of the historical and social identity of a particular town or village. However, many elements of folk religion that lingered into the early twentieth century have now been eclipsed and purged from ecclesiastical life, although residual elements may occasionally be encountered, particularly in attitudes to the rites of passage. Birth and death still seem to demand social recognition in some form of ritualised action and belief (Clark 1982:127) and continue to bring many people into affinity with the church.

However, the seasonal church calendar has continued to evolve. For example, many new memorial services and sermons locally abound. During the festive season, Christingle services are now common (see Chapter 6) and Crib and Toy Sunday services have appeared in many parishes in which toys are collected for disadvantaged children. Miracle plays have been revived in some areas and contemporary drama is frequently a feature in Sunday observances. No doubt many other new church initiatives will grow and foster their own customs according to local need. Conversely, at the threshold of the twenty-first century the institutional Church is facing many challenges in a hard-line secular world. Nevertheless, the impact of the ecclesiastic calendar and its seasonal influence on everyday community life should not be underestimated. In our contemporary world we may be on the threshold of a new reformation. There is a spiritual hunger takes which many forms, but a puritan ethic does not seem to be part of the agenda. Even in the secular world, it is becoming evident that sensibilities are turning to magic in the best sense of the word, that is, a desire for some kind of poetic re-enchantment of the world. Church customs and the festivals of the ritual year have a continuing role to play in this process.

Chapter Two

The People of the Church:
Privilege and Tradition

The people of faith are the body of the Church. From the very beginning of its institutional life, the Church has organised itself into a hierarchy of roles and responsibilities. Here we examine the duties of the faithful and the traditions that have developed around them. These include the devotional customs of the congregation, the privileges of the clergy and the activities of those who held the so-called 'minor offices'.

The Congregation

In English parish life there has often been a wry perception of the worshipping community. This has sometimes been expressed in gentle mocking humour as in this rhyme from Gloucestershire:

> Dirty Tredington, wooden steeple,
> Funny parson, wicked people.

(Simpson & Roud 2000: 67)

Despite local cynicism, which even modern congregations sometimes have to endure, the parishioners have always been the lifeblood of every parish church. Nevertheless, history reveals that becoming a member of a Church community has not always been down to individual choice. In the age of the Puritans, for example, attending church services was an obligation. The harsh laws of the time were believed to be a moral corrective against indifference, idleness and a perceived lack of religious principle. A fine was levied by the churchwardens for every non-attendance and the monies were used for the relief of the poor. Several Acts of Parliament were passed to try and ensure rigid observance of Sunday as a sacred day. An Act of 1676 specifically prohibited travelling, the pursuit of business, and all sales with the exception of milk. Even hanging out clothes to dry or taking a Sunday evening stroll were were considered to be misdmeanours and punishable with fines (Andrews 1891: 109; Roberts 1856: 238-246). Anyone caught tippling alcohol was severely punished by public whipping or a stint in the village stocks. Against this kind of legalistic background, many of the devotional customs probably evolved out of a sense of institutional coercion rather than natural devotion.

Dividing the sexes

Modern worshippers take it for granted that their gender is not an issue when attending an act of worship. However, one of the earliest impositions on church congregations was the practice of dividing the sexes, presumably because it was not considered seemly for men and women to be together in a sacred space. The custom dates back to the fourth century when the churches were divided into two portions by a barrier of wood. Generally, women went to the north side and men to the south side. This was still the conventional practice in the church at Helmsley, Yorkshire, as late as 1872 (Vaux 1894: 28). The practice of separation predictably met with disapproval and a couple who attempted to sit together in church at Abingdon in Oxfordshire were bluntly told: 'We don't have no sweathearting here!' (Smith 1971: 20). At Christ Church, Birmingham, this unwelcome segregation gave rise to a humorous doggerel:

> The churches and chapels we usually find
> Are places where men unto women are joined;
> But at Christ Church it seems they are more cruel-hearted,
> For men and their wives are brought there to be parted.

(Vaux 1894: 28)

Separate entrances to the church were provided in some parishes, and it was the custom for men to enter by the north door and in many churches up to the early nineteenth century this was known as the 'bachelors' door' (Vaux 1894: 29). In Somerset it is customary for the men to sit in front and the women behind. Hereford was the last cathedral where the sexes sat on different sides of the nave and, remarkably, the custom continued to the beginning of the twentieth century (Williamson 1923: 168). It was also a convention in some churches to give up the nave seats to the poor, the men sitting on both sides in the more eastern portion with the women behind them (Vaux 1894: 31).

Wearing hats and acts of reverence

No laws were prescribed for the dress of the congregation in British churches, as was the case in some parts of Europe. However, it was very much the custom before the reign of Charles I for men to wear hats in church. This trend lasted until long after the Reformation although it was often the focus of condemnation by senior clergy. It was usually the custom to remove hats upon entering the churchyard but always considered essential to remove headgear during a communion service when the Eucharistic host was being exhibited (Jefferson 1870 Vol 2: 26).

Most worshippers genuflect or 'acknowledge the altar' when they enter the nave, as an expression of reverence. In rural Yorkshire and elsewhere, it was usual for men to pluck their forelocks. It was always the custom there for the women to curtsey and the men to bow or touch their foreheads, when they entered and left the church. Making the sign of the cross on entering is an enduring practice because it acknowledges the sanctity of the church building, and recognises the presence of the Eucharistic elements. Crossing the chest is also undertaken at various points in the liturgy as a continual reminder of the Crucifixion and Resurrection. It has always been the practice to kneel in prayer upon first taking a seat in church. Even in the present, certain forms of churchmanship dictate that men will bow as the name of Jesus Christ is mentioned and women will curtsey at the same. Turning to the east at the Creeds is also a common devotional practice. There are of course, always some unexplained local oddities in the historical records. For example, at Churchdown in Gloucestershire it was the curious custom for the male labourers to stand during the sermon (*Notes and Queries* [1871] 8: 261); this is a practice not reported elsewhere.

Receiving Holy Communion

In the seventeenth century Communion would only be celebrated three times a year – Christmas, Easter and Whitsun. It is the central rite of the church and some worshippers fasted before communion and refused even to drink tea or coffee until after the Eucharistic service; these sensibilities are still followed by some Christians. Regional practices in church varied enormously and in some parishes men and women took Communion separately. Parishioners generally took Communion by order of social class, although at Swanage it is recorded that the twelve oldest men in the congregation went to the altar rail first (Smith 1971: 20). The communicants left their seats, went into the chancel and knelt down there, the men on the north and the women on the south side, and remained there until the priest came to offer them the Host. In Monmouthshire, Glamorganshire and parts of Herefordshire the tradition was for all those present to kneel through the whole of the Communion service. In Bristol churches even as late as the mid-nineteenth century it was commonplace for the men to stand during the Communion service till the reading of the Epistle (Vaux 1894: 64, 66). Many worshippers will also bow to the altar after receiving Communion.

We saw in Chapter 1 that all kinds of substances associated with the church and its rituals were popularly believed to be invested with powerful virtuous properties. The consecrated bread and wine were therefore deemed to have particularly efficacious properties. In pre-Reformation times for example, all manner of life problems could be rectified just by gazing at the host during Mass (Wilson 2004: 461). The official church policy has always dictated that any remnants of the Eucharistic elements should be reverently disposed of on consecrated ground, but the rinsings from the communion chalice were eagerly sought after by the sick (Opie and Tatum 1989: 93–94). Whooping cough was a worryingly frequent disease in earlier times and consecrated communion wine appears to have been much in demand as a folk-cure for this and other ailments (*Notes and Queries* [1882] 6: 387). Even old chalice veils have been recorded as desirable for bandaging burns (Wright 1913: 236).

The Clergy

The Shepherds of the flock of God

The church is conceived as 'priesthood of believers' but there has always been a need for spiritual leadership and management of parochial affairs. The reigning monarch has been the head of the Church of England and the next most powerful individual is the Archbishop of Canterbury as Primate of All England. However, it is the diocesan bishops under his jurisdiction who have a responsibility to provide local supervision, direction and leadership of the faithful. During the medieval period, the authority of a bishop made him a very powerful patriarchal figure. Bishops had their own farmed estates and, apart from their spiritual functions, they exercised powers almost identical to that of a wealthy manorial lord. However in spite of their considerable importance, few customs of have accrued around their offices and duties. The traditional observances were essentially intended to assert the bishop's authority. Typically this was reflected in the mandatory ringing of bells in his honour when he made a visitation within his diocese. A bishop is 'a shepherd of the flock' and his ancient office is symbolised by his crosier. His other distinctive emblem is the mitre with characteristic cords and ties which date back to the medieval period when bishops rode on horseback about their dioceses and their hats were liable to be blown off so were tied down by cords. However, it is the crosier that signifies his pastoral authority and he only uses this within his own territory. When a bishop takes office and arrives

The Bishop of Southwark announcing his arrival by knocking on the cathedral door. Photograph by James Hatt.

for his enthronement service, he traditionally announces his arrival by knocking three times on the cathedral door with his crosier. This symbolises that his authority is received by the people and that he is taking possession of the cathedral. He is then greeted by the Dean and formally welcomed.

The Parish Priest

In early Victorian England a parish clergyman was regarded as the archetypal gentleman and his parish status usually required that he was addressed as 'your reverence'. However, as noted in Chapter 1, historically, there have been ambivalent perceptions of the clergy and their role in public life, and to some extent the range of titles applied to them tend to reflect this. The title of 'parson' is simply 'the person', that is, the parish 'persona'. The more familiar designation of 'vicar' is really someone who undertook the work of the parish on behalf of another. The term is now used to describe the priest with responsibility for a parish. The word 'curate' once described the priest who had 'cure of souls' in his parish, but has lost some its original meaning and is now applied to the one who is in training and assists the parish priest (Williamson 1923: 166).

In some parishes the term 'rector' is encountered. The rector directly received 'tithes', that is, the 'tenth' of any designated local produce which was taken as a levy to sustain the church and help to supplement the his meagre earnings. Supplying the parish priest with provisions was always a priority in rural districts and it was a common Medieval practice to provide an area of land known as 'glebe' or the 'church furlong', which was set aside for this purpose. The tithing practice dates from an Anglo-Saxon law which required the laity to contribute to the upkeep of their church. All kinds of animal produce were given but wheat sheaves were the commonest offering and special tithe barns were built to accommodate them. Tithing was a frequent cause of ill-feeling, particularly after a bad harvest, and sometimes provoked riots. In Dorset it gave rise to the cynical saying 'just like the parson's barn', meaning a space that was never so full that it could not contain a little more (Baker 1974: 155). Inevitably, there were sustained attempts to evade the tithe, which have been suitably evoked in the words from a folk-song: 'We've cheated the Parson, we'll cheat him again!' (Smith 1971: 22).

The rector was essentially responsible for the repair of the chancel of his church because it is the part that is dedicated to the sacred offices and he was also charged to provide service books and vestments. The remainder of the building was the responsibility of the parish. There are few local variations in clergy descriptions but the Rector of the Church of St Blaise, Haccombe in Devon has the extraordinary exception of being known by the rare medieval title of 'archpriest'. The church was made a college or arch-presbytery in the early fourteenth century and was a community, comprising an arch-priest and five clerics. The church has no particular privileges, but the title still stands and is unique in the Church of England. Another interesting anomaly recorded at the end of the nineteenth century was the title 'Lord Rector' as belonging to a clergyman. Like rectors, they owned tithes but had position and responsibilities almost equivalent to manorial lords. Only six lord rectors were recorded in Victorian England (Vaux 1894: 182).

Clergy privileges

Unusual legal rights prevailed for the clergy both before and after the Reformation. Until 1429, all priests were free from arrest and prosecution for any crime including murder. This privilege was known as 'benefit of clergy' and to prove their right to it they had to read Psalm 51, which became known as the 'neck verse', in order to escape punishment (Andrews 1900:13). Conversely, it is also true that anyone in Holy Orders cannot serve on a jury and is disqualified from sitting in the House of Commons. The special exemptions of clergy also appeared to allow them to transcend

Christian morals in the popular mind. A widespread belief, which prevailed until the seventeenth century, maintained that the parson could authorise the killing of aged parents who had become a burden to the family. A special cosh or 'church mawle' was even provided for this purpose! (Aubrey 1881: 127).

Unlike their modern counterparts, medieval priests had few dispensations in daily life and most clergy lived in destitution. The 'inferior clergy' in London were described as 'objects of extreme wretchedness', dressed in tattered cassocks and living in garrets (Stackhouse 1737: 3). The common fee for a sermon was a shilling and a dinner, and for reading prayers, twopence and a cup of coffee. However, given their reduced circumstances, parishioners could be generous towards their clerics and it was customary in many parishes to offer them food and wine at the close of morning service, especially for guest preachers (Vaux 1894: 186).

Hostile attitudes to clergy

The clergy have not always been popular with their parishioners and past attitudes have sometimes been remarkably hostile. A 'gentleman parson' might also have a second office as a local magistrate and clerical justices were particularly disliked. However, the tithing custom undoubtedly generated the greatest strength of anticlerical feeling in rural districts. A prudent incumbent would know that he could moderate the resentful feelings of the farming community by holding a tithe-audit dinner. These were jovial occasions where hearty food and drink was served in great quantity and eaten energetically by farmers used to much more frugal offerings. Parson Francis Kilvert records in his diaries just such an occasion at his parish in Brentwardine, Herefordshire, in 1878 where fifty tithe-payers joined him for a generous dinner of turkey, roast beef, jugged hare and beefsteak pie, followed by an exorbitant range of sweet puddings, cheese and fruit (Kilvert 1944: 324–5). In the same charitable spirit, 'tithe breakfasts' were also held in Eastbourne, Sussex on the first three Sundays of August and for every wagon owned by the farm, two servants attended a similar repast in the barn (Wolesley 1921: 229).

The ambivalent attitudes to the clergy since medieval times gave rise to a variety of disapproving superstitions. For example, ships' chaplains or clergy holiday-makers have often been vigorously shunned on board ship by sailors as their presence can mean bad weather or lead to some other misfortune (*Notes and Queries* [1854] 10: 26). Fishermen on the way to joining their boat were always afraid of meeting a clergyman, and factory girls from the Staffordshire potteries would quickly touch iron if they met a priest on the road (Witcutt 1941: 237). This unsympathetic outlook could partly be accounted for by the black attire worn by the clergy and its consequent association with death.

Although clerics could receive indifferent or hostile treatment there was at least one unruly tradition that was played out in a more light-hearted spirit. The ancient custom of 'crabbing the parson' was an annual occurrence at Kenelstowe, Staffordshire, on St Kenelm's Day (17 July), when the villagers celebrated with a village fair known as 'St Kenelm's Wake' They would proceed to the church of St Kenelm and bombard the unfortunate cleric with a volley of crab apples. This boisterous event was apparently undertaken to commemorate the activities of an unscrupulous local parson who stole some dumplings from a farmhouse on his way to church which he duly secreted in the sleeves of his surplice. Whilst the parson was later reading the service in church, the dumplings fell out and hit the clerk on the head. The clerk duly retaliated by pelting the parson with some crab apples that he conveniently had to hand (Brand 1849 Vol 1: 344). Unfortunately, the use of crab apples gave way to more dangerous missiles such as sticks and stones which soon led to the tradition being suppressed and eventually dying out by the early nineteenth century.

The Parish Clerk

The office of the church that was next in line to the incumbent was the parish clerk. This is not however, to be confused with the modern local government role of the clerk to the parish council. The clerk was one of the minor orders of the church and in his original role he had to discharge a formidable array of responsibilities. During the medieval period, the clerk was immediately recognisable in a church setting by his distinctive tonsure; the crown of his head was shaven in monastic fashion, so that all remaining hair resembled a circle of thorns around his head in remembrance of the Crown of Thorns. His primary function was to assist in the services, and arrange the music of the church. Specific liturgical functions ranged through singing the responses, reading lessons and giving out the hymns to proclaiming marriage banns, serving at the altar and cleaning the vestments and sacred vessels. Sprinkling holy water was one of the clerks particularly important liturgical duties because of the powerful purifying effects that were attributed to holy water in popular belief. Younger clerks were often known as 'holy water clerks' and they were given the privilege of carrying water around country parishes as well as leading processions (Christie 1893: 5, 14). The clerk was also charged with more menial duties such as opening up the church, ringing the bell and, if no sexton was appointed, he would also dig the graves. It was frequently the clerk who published all parish notices concerning both religious and secular matters. Parish clerks were often the focus of all kinds of local church customs and sometimes received special privileges; some of these are described elsewhere in this book.

To be worthy of being a parish clerk the candidate had, according to a seventeenth century canon, 'to be at least twenty years old. Known to the parson as a man of honest conversation and sufficient for his reading, writing and keeping accounts, competent skill in singing' (Ditchfield 1907: 245). Their reading skills could be in great demand as exemplified by a strange custom observed at Hexham, Northumberland. Here it was common for the cattle traders to carry all letters received in the course of their trade to the parish church, where the clerk read them aloud after the service, and answered them according to individual need (Legg 1905: xlv). There are a number of accounts of clerks who were tone deaf and others who amusingly muddled their verbal deliveries in reading lessons and giving notices (Ditchfield 1907: 58-61), but these were the exceptions and the clerk's role was always considered essential to the smooth running of the church. They were often held in great affection by parishioners and sometimes received many gifts and money, such as eggs and cakes and sheaves of corn.

The office of parish clerk was essentially a male role, often handed down from father to son. Until the end of the eighteenth century a woman could not legally be elected to this position although she could take the role of a sexton and was known as a 'sextoness'. However, by the nineteenth century records start to show women being admitted to the post. After the Reformation many of the minor offices disappeared and the clerk would potentially have widened his role to incorporate the offices of sexton, reader, acolyte and sub-deacon. For all of the diversity and weight of responsibility, the remuneration of a parish clerk was never substantial. The need to augment their meagre salary led to some clerks scandalously allowing visitors to take away fragments of stained glass or church fabric (Neale 1846: 19), presumably for superstitious purposes, in exchange for a small sum of money. A more legitimate custom for boosting their income was to hold a 'clerk ale' – see Chapter 4.

The Worshipful Company of Parish Clerks

The ancient lineage of the parish clerk as a lay office can be traced back to 1232 when a London Guild of Parish Clerks existed. The fraternity developed into the fellowship that is now known as the Worshipful Company of Parish Clerks, receiving its first charter in 1442. It was constituted to have a responsibility to all of the parishes within the City of London, and selected parishes outside its boundary, which remains to this day. The company has been housed in three halls within the City of London during its long history, the last and third hall being destroyed by enemy action in December 1940.

The Master of the Parish Clerks Company wearing his crown. Photograph by Tiggy Coombes.

The Master of the Company is elected at an early meeting of the court on Ascension Day and holds office for one year. In the evening after a church service, the company brethren, wearing white surplices, move in procession to a nearby Livery hall where they sit down to an election dinner. During the dinner an elaborately embroidered crown is used by the past Master to ensure that the 'right person' has been elected to this office by establishing a 'good fit'.

A unique aspect of the company fellowship is the custom of brethren referring to each other by the names of their churches. This manifests itself spectacularly when the toasts at dinner are proposed and drunk and the unique custom of 'cross toasting' begins. A clerk will stand and raise his glass calling, for example, 'St Thomas Apostle!' and a response might be 'St Dunstan in the West!' Thereafter a vociferous exchange of parish names continues for several minutes. In the present era, not all members of the Company are working as parish clerks in the traditional sense, but all members serve their parishes or the wider church with a diversity of roles and responsibilities.

Verger and sexton

In rural churches the duties of clerk and sexton were usually performed by the same person. Where a sexton was appointed, he generally had an assistant function to the clerk. This was not an elected position as he was regarded a servant of the parish rather than an officer. In recent times the office of sexton has merged with that of verger. The verger, like the clerk, usually assisted in services as he does today, by escorting the clergy at cathedral services. He carries a ceremonial rod known as a 'virge' (from the Latin *virga*, branch, staff or rod) which in former times may have been pressed into service to hold back animals or fend off an overexcited crowd from the person he was escorting, or even used to discipline disobedient choristers! Sextons by contrast, carried out the more menial duties around the church and churchyard but had a primary responsibility for grave-digging and tolling the 'passing bell'. One of the most notorious bell customs to be performed by a sexton took place in the City of London up to the end of the eighteenth century. The sexton of the Church of St Sepulchre had the mournful task of tolling a hand bell outside Newgate prison the night before the execution of the condemned criminals, and afterwards he repeated these words:

> All you that in the condemned hold do lie,
> Prepare you, for to-morrow you shall die:
> Watch all and pray; the hour is drawing near
> That you before the Almighty must appear:
> Examine well yourselves; in time repent,
> That you may not to eternal flames be sent:
> And when St Sepulchre's bell tomorrow tolls,
> The Lord above have mercy on your souls!

When a parishioner died, one of the important tasks of a sexton was to inform a local 'searcher' whose duty it was to visit the deceased and ascertain the cause of death. They were usually elderly women who had no medical knowledge, and therefore their diagnosis could only have been very conjectural. They were charged with reporting their findings to the parish clerk, but records suggest that these were scanty and inaccurate. Many sextons and indeed some clerks were of dubious character and poorly educated, which meant that they could be unreliable and were sometimes caught up in illegal pursuits. There are several accounts of clerks and sextons in Cornwall who were involved in smuggling and wrecking activities and even parish priests were known to collude in these illicit dealings (Ditchfield 1896: 83–6).

Churchwardens

The churchwarden has always been an important lay officer of the church. This was a position originally held by men, but as with the parish clerks, attitudes gradually changed and the first records of women taking this office date from the end of the nineteenth century. Churchwardens always had a duty to look after maintenance of the church buildings and produce an inventory of the valuables. In former times they also had a duty to keep meticulous financial accounts. Churchwardens have a particular responsibility for keeping the peace within the church precincts and often worked in conjunction with parish constables. The symbol of their office is the warden's 'stave' which is used in ceremonial procession but in earlier times it would have been used as staff to fend of unruly persons or intruders.

Their onerous duties also included a responsibility to monitor the moral behaviour of parishioners and call to account anyone who stepped out of line. This obligation effectively required churchwardens to have a policing role with full powers of arrest within church grounds. At Manchester, for example, at the close of the nineteenth century it was the custom for the chief magistrate of the town, with the churchwardens and police officers, to leave the church after the first lesson, and to compel all persons found in the streets to come into the church or pay a fine. In a similar judicial spirit, in the parishes of the West Riding of Yorkshire customarily churchwardens left the morning service just after the banns had been published; they would then visit the public-houses near the churchyard to see that all was quiet and return to the church in time for the sermon. They were not always conscientious in discharging this duty, as reported in 1872 when the churchwardens of one Yorkshire parish got into trouble when the police found them drinking in a public-house which they had visited officially during morning service (Vaux 1894: 193). Churchwardens had the task of looking out for intoxicated members of the congregation during the service and anyone who was found to be drunk and disorderly in church could face a few hours in the public stocks. Although magistrates would administer legal punishments, churchwardens had the right to deal directly with offenders without recourse to legal officialdom. The last instance of stocks being used by churchwardens for punishing drunken behaviour during divine service was at Newbury, Berkshire, as late as 1872 (Andrews 1900: 187). Churchwardens still, in theory, have a policing role but the more punitive elements of their office are no longer enforced.

Dogs and dog-whippers

From the sixteenth to nineteenth centuries dogs were liable to be a particular nuisance during church services. Most dogs were simply strays but hens, chickens and other animals could also be frequent intruders. If dogs became disruptive during the service it was the job of the appointed 'dog whipper' or 'dog-noper' to remove them from the church. This role was sometimes undertaken by the clerk, sexton or even the parish beadle, but the responsibility was also an official church appointment that was retained by many churches well into the nineteenth century. They would bear a long peeled willow wand, fashioned as whip although in some parishes extendable 'dog tongs' up to a length of eight feet were used. An original dog whip is still displayed in St Anne's Church, Baslow in Derbyshire. The most curious story concerning an unwelcome dog in a church service originates from York Minster where it is said that a dog once swallowed the consecrated wafer on St Luke's Day (18 October). Annually on that day it was customary to whip every dog in the vicinity so it eventually became known as Dog Whipping Day (Brewer 1898: 367–8).

Money was sometimes bequeathed to provide for the office of the dog whipper and in some rural areas a piece of the village land was made available for his use. For example, at Cleverley, Shropshire, a rent of ten shillings a year was paid by a tenant on lands called 'Dogwhippers Marsh', 'to a person for keeping order in the church during divine service' (Edwards 1842: 222). In some parishes, the dog-whipper had his own pew, a surviving example of which can be seen at St Margaret's Church, Wrenbury, Cheshire. Dog whippers became less common from the late eighteenth century onwards, presumably because parishes increasingly made it clear that animals were unwelcome at church services. One of the last recorded dog-whippers was appointed to Exeter Cathedral in 1856 and a small room over the North Porch of the cathedral is still known as the Dog Whipper's Flat (Brewer 1898: 368).

Noisy boys and sleeping parishioners

Unruly dogs were not the only concern during divine service and it was often necessary to take a stern line with rowdy boys in the congregation. At the Collegiate Church of Wolverhampton, an annual bequest of five shillings was left by Richard Brooke to employ a man to keep the boys quiet during the services and no doubt this custom was a fairly general practice (Tyack 1899: 115). Of equal concern was the tendency of parishioners to fall asleep during the sermon. This was a common occurrence, especially in rural areas where many people had worked six days in the fields and by Sunday, were physically exhausted. Inevitably, this was regarded as irreverent behaviour and a church official was charged with the job of waking them up. The role was occasionally an additional duty of the dog-whipper although more usually it fell to the lot of the parish beadle. At St Peter's, Coventry, dozing parishioners were roused by a 'whippy cane' (Palmer 1976: 39), while at

Dunchurch, Warwickshire, a 'sluggard-waker' was employed to prod sleepers with a fork-shaped piece of wood (Andrews 1890b: 175). In Warrington, Lancashire, the appointee was known as a 'bobber' in reference to his long stick with a bob fastened on the end of it (Dyer 1891: 64). If the beadle undertook this duty he was usually equipped with a long staff, which in Warwickshire was fitted with a brass knob at one end and a fox's brush at the other. Inattentive working people received a tap with the brass knob, while the aristocracy 'were given a tactful twitch with the brush' (Palmer 1976: 39).

Choristers and Boy Bishops

Choristers have always been at the very heart of the liturgical life of cathedrals in the ancient monastic tradition of singing daily services. They also came to have increasing importance in parish churches, as indeed they do in the present. The traditions that have accrued around choristers tend to focus on particular events and customs such as beating the bounds or memorial events, rather than any special acts associated with liturgical practice. Many of these traditions will be found throughout this book. However, an unusual cathedral custom was the taking of 'spur money'. The choir boys, in accordance with an ancient custom, claimed a fine of five shillings from any military man wearing his spurs during divine service. This was recorded at St George's Chapel, Windsor Castle, as late as 1898 and records are also known from St Paul's Cathedral, Westminster Abbey, and elsewhere. Spurs were clearly singled out for particular disapproval and along with hats, were also banned from many church belfries (Walcott 1872: 90-91; Andrews 1900: 148-151).

Without doubt, one of the most intriguing ecclesiastical practices must be the ceremonial election of a chorister to the role of Boy Bishop. Its origins can be traced to the Roman feast of Saturnalia which occurred between 16 and 23 December, a time of universal merry-making when moral and class restrictions were temporarily relaxed. There was clearly an element of festive subversion and role-reversal. However, in the early medieval period, childhood was regarded as an unimportant transitory stage of life so the imagery of the Boy Bishop helped to educate people into a deeper awareness of children in the Divine Scheme (Mackenzie 1987: 10–11). Furthermore, in pre-Reformation times, when bishops were regarded as powerful religious and secular figures, occasional surges of anti-clerical feeling could be briefly moderated by temporarily witnessing them being deprived of their authority.

The practice of electing a boy bishop spread throughout Western Europe and was common in most cathedrals as well as colleges, grammar schools, and

Boy Bishop enthroned at Hereford Cathedral. Photograph by Hereford Cathedral .

parish churches. The origins of the service are uncertain, but the custom of choosing a Boy Bishop is thought to date from the thirteenth century. Following his election, the chorister was dressed in full bishop's robes, and given a mitre and crosier and would ceremonially take his place on the bishop's throne to receive a blessing. In the medieval ceremony, the cathedral clergy would give up their seats to the choristers and take those places normally occupied by the choir. The enthronement always took place on St Nicholas' Day (6 December) to commemorate the saint's compassion towards children. The Boy Bishop continued to hold office until Holy Innocents Day (28 December), which was regarded as the choristers' special day, when he was expected to give a sermon. During this period he enjoyed many of the powers and privileges of a bishop, which included officiating at all cathedral services with the exception of the Mass. The Boy Bishop would also be engaged in collecting and distributing money for charitable causes or for the enjoyment of himself and his attendants. Sometimes the celebrations could degenerate into unruly behaviour and the whole period of office could witness a good deal of boyish merriment and pranks. Their riotous behaviour sometimes became offensive and eventually led to Henry VIII banning their election in English churches in 1542 and their final abolition came under Elizabeth I.

Boy Bishop enthroned at Hereford Cathedral. Photograph by Hereford Cathedral .

The enthroning of the Boy Bishop has seen a revival in recent years and has been annually celebrated on 6 December with particular enthusiasm at Hereford Cathedral since 1982. The enthronement follows a simple service which has been adapted from the medieval Hereford and Salisbury rites with the addition of a toy collection for charity at the end. Boy Bishop revivals have also occurred at Berden, Hertfordshire; Boston, Lincolnshire; Par, Cornwall and Edwinstone, Nottinghamshire (Day 1999: 162) and Salisbury Cathedral.

The bell-ringers

Church ringers were regarded as one of the most important groups in a local community and by the eighteenth century, the art and popularity of ringing had grown to the extent that England was known proverbially as the 'ringing Island' (Warne 1969: 58). Bells were generally rung by deacons in pre-Reformation times but later, fraternities of lay ringers were formed. By the 1890s the ringers were independent of any governing authorities, practising and controlling their work in a manner similar to the craft guilds of the period

The oldest depiction of a bell-ringer known in England. Part of the decoration on a twelfth century chancel arch at Stoke Dry, Rutland. The bell is simply mounted on a wooden post with a cantilevered arm. Photograph by Bob Trubshaw .

(Bushaway 1982: 51). Bell-ringing is tiring, physical work, and ringers were generally rewarded well with food and drink after a long peal. Large quantities of beer were provided in barrels and drunk from leather jugs or 'jacks', which could be of considerable size and were a common feature in church towers (Camp 1988: 53; Andrews 1895: 74–7).

Food was usually provided as a gratuity, and in Nottinghamshire villages, commemorative marks incised on the walls of the belfry were known as 'cakes' or 'cheeses' after the customary refreshments offered on these occasions (Baker 1974: 163–4). Bell ringers spent a good deal of time together and their fraternal culture is touchingly expressed in an ancient tradition at St George's Church, Great Bromley, Essex. Here it is still the

Bell-ringers hats at St George's Church, Great Bromley, Essex. Photograph by Mark Lewis.

custom for deceased bell-ringers to have their hats hung high in the church below the belfry. This tradition seems to go back at least to the early eighteenth century and one of the hats is dated 1716 (Kent 2005: 114). When a bell-ringer died it was generally the custom in many places for a 'dumb' or 'muffled peal' to be rung (Baker 1974: 164). Bell-ringing customs are further explored in Chapter 3.

Chapter Three

The Church and Churchyard:
Customs and Superstitions

Walking towards a church takes you through bands of sacredness. These begin at the border of the church grounds, becoming stronger towards the church building itself. This progression of sacred power has inevitably had a significant impact on popular belief. Sacred space has always possessed a potency which has blurred the boundaries between devotion and spiritual belief on the one hand and the realm of magic on the other. Nevertheless, consecrated ground is also public space and as a result, churches have often been used for secular activities that sometimes crossed the line into subversion and sacrilege. Here we will explore the diverse religious and secular uses of the church and its precincts, and the beliefs associated with its fabric.

The building of the church

Even though church buildings are sanctified and the ground on which they are built is consecrated, medieval parishioners still felt a pressing need to protect them with objects and symbols that functioned as charms and amulets. These protective measures began at the earliest building stage with the laying of the foundations. The tradition of offering a human sacrifice to ensure the stability of a building was widespread in many cultures and a number of significant discoveries suggest this was a common custom among early church builders. Skeletons found under the walls of churches at Brownsover in Warwickshire have been considered as sacrifices for this purpose (Gomme 1883: 34-35) and there are many other examples scattered

The Cheese Rolling at Randwick, Gloucestershire. Photograph by Clive and Sheila Bliss.

in the literature of folklore. Stonework from earlier pagan structures was also incorporated into parts of the church building and may have served to deflect evil influences by association with their original function (Eaton 2000: 99). In part, these actions may have been an expression of transitional belief during the Anglo-Saxon period when churches were built on pagan sites and pagan beliefs were still very prominent in the collective mind.

Other forms of protective device have also been discovered in the fabric of church buildings. Margaret Baker (Baker 1974: 166) suggests that the occasional practice of workmen scratching shoes and foot shapes on lead church roofs may have had a protective function as well as the intention to leave a mark of identification. She also cites the discovery of lead 'footprints' found during repairs at Nether Worton Church, Oxfordshire. Branches of rowan were considered to be a powerful protection against witchcraft and built into church walls (Baker 1974: 165). Candles and eggs have also been found embedded in church walls and foundations, suggesting later substitutes for human or animal sacrifice (Andrews 1899: 42–3). Weathercocks on church spires were also believed to guard the church precincts and crow on Doomsday to wake the dead and drive away the powers of darkness (Opie and Tatem 1989: 90–1; Ettlinger 1967: 279).

A unique custom that still takes place at St John's Church, Randwick, on the first Sunday in May is traditionally considered to ward off evil spirits in the coming year. Three double Gloucester cheeses are blessed at the altar before being rolled around the church three times anticlockwise. One of the cheeses is cut up and share among the congregation, while the remaining cheeses form part of a procession held on the following Saturday. This event was revived in 1972.

Protecting the church door

The entrance of the church has inevitably been regarded as the part in need of greatest protection. The western door was regarded as especially vulnerable, requiring very strong safeguards. One suggestion is that this developed from an ancient belief that the seat of demons is in the west (Ettlinger 1962: 163). Horseshoes, which are more familiar on domestic buildings and gates, were frequently displayed on church doors to ward off evil spirits – and sometimes buried under the doorsteps. Robert Lawrence observes that crescent-shaped pieces of metal were sometimes nailed up at the entrances of churches as protective emblems. He considers that the horseshoe was an easily available substitute for the 'halo', combining its function with the pagan belief that horseshoes were an effective protection against malevolent spirits (Lawrence 1898: 121–2). Sometimes small votive crosses may be found scratched or incised into the jambs of church doors and elsewhere in the church, notably in Buckinghamshire. Ellen Ettlinger suggests that these may have been 'invocations for help', presumably of a spiritual nature (Ettlinger 1967: 280).

The need to protect the church building from malign influences also extended to the external walls of the whole building. Gargoyles (from the Latin *gurgulio*, meaning 'throat') are one of the most striking external features and they have the practical function of throwing rainwater clear of the church. But their fantastic and monstrous forms have given rise to various symbolic interpretations. Many are comical, some are terrifying, others bawdy. Symbolic meanings can be over-zealously applied as these carvings may have simply been the whimsical and spontaneous expressions of local stone carvers. In popular church lore their primary purpose is to scare away the Devil, although in a more homiletic spirit they have also been understood as contrasting the external profane world with the holy sanctuary to be found within.

In popular belief, the sanctity of the church building conferred all kinds of blessings and virtuous properties upon the fabric and sacred objects contained within. Dust, lead or stone were all believed to carry blessings and be effective against malign influences or troublesome ailments. So for example, heart-shaped pendants made from lead scrapings which had been taken from church windows were considered an effective cure for sore breasts while dust brought from the floor of the church was taken to the bed of the dying to ease a lingering death (Tyack 1899: 124).

The church porch

The church porch has always been regarded as an ambiguous space by parishioners, and in medieval times it did not hold the same degree of holiness as the church building (Postles 2007). During the medieval period, when municipal buildings were virtually absent, the church porch became an important public domain for visibly and openly settling debts, legacies of wills, rents and other financial obligations. Courts of justice also took place there. The south door was favoured for the porch and the proximity to the sacred space of the church would have given a certain gravitas to these secular proceedings. Local tradesmen sold their products there and consequently benches were provided on both sides of the porch. In some localities, the porch also functioned as a temporary mortuary and dead bodies were laid there for identification (Vaux 1894: 25). Secular uses certainly dominated this part of the churchyard although, in pre-modern times, the greater part of the marriage service was conducted in the church porch – see Chapter 8.

The right of sanctuary

An intriguing function of the church door relates to the ancient privilege of 'sanctuary'. This was accorded to persons who had committed a crime which demanded death, and who were able to reach a church or other privileged place before they were apprehended. Several cathedrals were granted this right which seems to have been primarily associated with the north door wherever the privilege was known. As soon as a fugitive grasped the handle, that person could not be removed without 'breaking sanctuary'. There are notable examples of heavy knockers at Hexham Abbey, Northumberland, St Gregory's, Norwich, and Durham Cathedral which have traditionally believed to have been associated with the right of sanctuary. Typically, at Durham a bell was tolled to signal the fact that a man had taken sanctuary and the refugee was provided with food, drink and bedding for up to thirty-seven days (Andrews 1891: 12–13). Some cathedrals provided 'sanctuary chairs' in which a criminal was guaranteed protection. A fine Saxon example survives at Beverley Minster, Yorkshire, where it is known as the 'Frid stool' or 'chair of peace'. The right of sanctuary was finally abolished in 1624 (Vaux 1894: 22).

The 'Frid Stool' at Beverley Minster. Photograph by Mervyn King.

The church interior

The font

Traditionally the font (Latin *fons*, 'fountain') was always placed by the west door as it symbolises entry into the Church and the Christian fellowship. As the Church consolidated and spread the font was first developed for full immersion. Then, as infant baptism became more common, fonts became smaller, although many examples from the medieval period were large enough for the full immersion of an infant. The Canons of the Church ordered that fonts should be made of stone; free-standing vessels of plaster or earthenware were considered illegal (Andrews 1895:82) probably because they would be easily removable and taken away for private use or superstitious purposes. In many fonts, marks indicating the former presence of a protective lock and cover are common. The baptismal customs associated with the font are explored in Chapter 7.

The altar and chancel

The altar or communion table is the heart of the church and a focus of liturgical activities. The chancel or sanctuary in which it stands is also the most sacred domain of the church, although during the medieval period, the altar was the setting for a variety of secular transactions. Land sales, rents and mortgages were paid there and oaths were often legally sanctioned and taken at the altar. No doubt, like the church porch, this hallowed space conferred a certain solemnity and possibly even greater seriousness to the proceedings. Even as late as 1762 the altar was where parishioners in some districts left small tithes, such as milk, butter and cheese just before worship began (Addy 1913: 194–6).

By virtue of its central function in liturgy, and the celebration of the Eucharist in particular, the altar or communion table was deemed to possess the most efficacious magical powers. There was, for example, a belief that fits could be cured by walking around or creeping under the altar three times, no doubt in the name of the Trinity (Bray 1838 Vol II: 291). In Devon, persons suffering from fits were advised to go to the parish church at midnight on 23 June, and walk through each aisle, then crawl three times from north to south under the communion table exactly as the clock strikes twelve (Hewett 1892: 46).

Pews and their customs

One of the most intriguing facets of church lore is the development of the pew. Up to the beginning of the Reformation, the naves of churches were to a great extent devoid of seating and were simply large, open spaces. At this time the aged and infirm used portable stools (Vaux 1894: 13) although many churches provided stone benches for their use along the inside walls and this is the undoubtedly the origin of phrase 'the weak going to the wall'. The introduction of pews for the convenience of worshippers was very gradual, but increased with the rise of the sermon as a central act of Christian worship. They were originally purchased from the church by private individuals or families, and whole ranges of pews or seats were erected in accordance with the position or wealth of the occupants. The seats for the poor were mockingly referred to as the 'free seats' and were always uncomfortable and hidden away from the main body of the church (Beresford 1874: 17). Pews were also allotted for particular officers of the church including the clerk and churchwardens. The local squire also had his own designated pew and use of the 'The Hall Dog Pew', a compartment in which his dog could be accommodated during the service. Examples of these are known from churches in Aveley in Essex and Northorpe, Lincolnshire (Vaux 1894: 15; Hardman 1890: 27).

Box pews became fashionable because they provided privacy and allowed a family to sit together. Some were built to absurd heights and this trend was encouraged by the Puritans, for it not only offered seclusion but could also proclaim pride and conceal irreverent behaviour (Jeafferson Vol 2: 14). The abuse of pews continued and by the seventeenth century they could include windows, curtains, sofas, cushions, tables, fireplaces and other material comforts. For the aristocracy, the tedium of a long service could also be relieved by the entry of a servant with sherry and light refreshments. There were often bitter disputes about 'ownership' and occupation of seats in churches and many legal discussions ensued about the appropriateness of acquiring space and possession of seats in church with the consequent social divisions that this publicly reinforced.

The most intriguing annual custom of 'Flapping the Church' occurred at Otteringham in the East Riding of Yorkshire up to early nineteenth century. On the evening of 5 November every boy in the parish tied a stout piece of leather about six inches long to a length of cord and then went to the church, led by the parish clerk. As soon as they were gathered inside the church, the ringers started a peal. The clerk then shouted out, 'Now, boys, flap away!' and then all the pews in the church were thrashed inside and out by the flappers. Having flogged the pews for some time, the leather weapons were generally at the end directed against each other, and the whole ceremony closed with a general chase around the sacred building. A similar observance also took place nearby at Skirlaugh and at Roose, where it was curiously known as 'Babbling' (*Notes and Queries* [1858] 5: 236). The custom would appear to be an outlet for youthful energy and high spirits, and its occurrence on Guy Fawkes' Night may be significant, although it has never been adequately explained.

The secular uses of church buildings

In the medieval period the space and weather-tight roof of a country church was particularly useful for storing perishable goods and farm products such as wool. This was generally a happy arrangement supported by the local clergy who received small payments of money from the owners of the goods. Gradually, churches became the settings for all kinds of secular activities. The nave was generally the focus for most encounters and it frequently served as a church hall where the parishioners could gather in relative comfort. In the big cities, cathedrals were widely recognised as areas for a variety of social transactions. The naves of a great many of these buildings, such as St Paul's, Durham, Norwich Cathedral and York Minster were all public thoroughfares where it was fashionable to see and be seen (Vaux 1894: 3). Much of this social intercourse took place with decorum but, especially during seasonal festivals, there was growing concern about buying and selling in the sacred buildings. In pre-Reformation times the nave was the place where tradesmen bartered and where owners of property deposited their goods. The nave of St Paul's and Durham Cathedrals for example, were especially notorious as the venue of usurers and horse dealers. Parish churches could witness busy gatherings, where all kinds of dealers might appear both in the church and the churchyard, openly spreading their wares on the tombstones (Andrews 1895: 148).

Lawyers also had interviews with their clients in churches, which were widely used as courts of justice and for manorial courts (Vaux 1894: 2-3; Jefferson 1870: 339). In fact, Addy persuasively suggests a Christian origin for the twelve men of a jury in the presence of a judge as a parallel to Christ and the twelve disciples (Addy 1898: 176). The consistory courts were held in churches for centuries and, prior to 1840, they had jurisdiction over the crimes of clerks as well as matrimonial and probate matters. Some churches even had a brush with local politics and there were instances of the buildings being used in the nineteenth century for proposing and seconding parliamentary candidates (Vaux 1894: 10–11).

An interesting civic connection still occurs at All Saints Church, Brightlingsea in Essex on 'Choosing Day'. This port traditionally took its authority from the Cinque Port of Sandwich in Kent, and on the first Monday after St Andrew's Day (1 December) after a short service, the 'Deputy of Brightlingsea', who represents the Mayor of Sandwich, is ceremonially elected on the steps of the chancel in the presence of Cinque port dignitaries.

Lively entertainments also took place within the church and precincts. Dancing seems to have been occasionally tolerated as joyful celebration. George Tyack quotes John Aubrey writing in 1686, who remarked that dancing in church after prayers during the Christmas holidays was the ancient custom in Yorkshire (Tyack 1899: 117). Sometimes, behaviour in the church could take a particularly indecent turn and even Sir Thomas More recorded his disgust that women were found profanely singing ribald songs in procession within the cathedrals (Tyack 1899: 118). In pre-modern times the public were occasionally entertained by the performances of acrobats on ropes strung between steeples and nearby buildings, as occurred at St Paul's Cathedral on the coronation of Edward VI (Andrews 1891: 244). Trying to suppress these activities became a great concern of the Reformers and Henry VIII launched an injunction that no person should abuse the churches by eating, drinking, buying, selling, playing or dancing. But even this was unable to check the prevailing licence (Vaux 1894: 4). Wakes, Whitsun ales and other revelries thrived; these are discussed in Chapter 5.

The church tower, clock and bells

The church tower is the most visible part of a church and intended to communicate a visible Christian witness to the parish. The church clock had special significance because it was usually the only timepiece in a village community and visible for a considerable distance. It also served symbolically to remind the faithful that the flight of time was a call to prepare for eternity. So it is not surprising that the mournful striking church clock would come to have dark omens associated with it. For example, if the clock struck while a lesson was being read or a hymn was being sung, a death would follow in the parish that week (Baker 1974: 165). If the church clock struck the hour during a wedding, the bride or groom would die within a year, although if the timing was such that the bride heard the chime while still outside the church, then good luck could follow (Simpson and Roud 2000: 71). Superstitious practices concerning the tower itself are few, but an unsettling example from Lydford, Devon, is worthy of mention. The parish clerk received a small gratuity for carrying children afflicted with 'the thrush' up the church tower, where he would hold them over the battlements at each pinnacle while he recited the Lord's Prayer (Baring-Gould 1900: 126).

Church tower customs

Two interesting customs take place on Oak Apple Day (29 May) which both make use of the visible height provided by a church tower. The first is the preservation of woodcutting rights in Grovely Forest near Wishford Magna, Salisbury, Wiltshire. After a procession to Grovely Forest to collect branches of oak, four women lead a group to Salisbury Cathedral to present branches to the Dean at 10 a.m.. There is then a return procession to Wishford Magna church where an oak bough is hoisted to the top of the tower. This is known as the 'Marriage Bough' and is believed to ensure fertility for all couples married at the church during the following year.

A similar custom takes place on the same day at Castleton, Derbyshire, on Oak Apple Day, supposedly in remembrance of Charles II. After touring the village pubs on horseback accompanied by his queen, a procession and a band, a mock Stuart 'king' is relieved of his garland, known as the 'Queen', which is then hoisted up to the top of the tower of St Edmunds Church, where it is left to wither. (Andrews 1891: 177–85; Addy 1901: 394–428). Other seasonal tower customs are described in Chapter 4.

Bell-ringing customs and superstitions

The main function of the church tower was to house the bells. Bells have always been an important medium of both secular and religious communication since the early medieval period. According to the canons of the church, parishioners were only required to provide one bell, but a complement of five was not unusual in many parishes. Bells were often the most favoured gifts to churches from benefactors who wished to be remembered, so the installation of new bells was usually a cause for much celebration and lively 'bell wakes' were held in many villages.

The bells were tolled primarily to call parishioners to a daily service. Ringing patterns and timings varied considerably across the country. On Sundays, bells were always rung for Matins, Holy Communion and Evensong. This custom, to varying degrees, continues into the present. Bells were also tolled to give warning of different parts of the service. The 'sermon bell' was to give notice that a sermon was about to be given. The 'sanctus' or 'saunce' bell was rung when the priest began the Sanctus in the Office of the Mass; three strokes were given on the bell so that the sick and others absent from the church, could all join in this song of adoration. This custom is still maintained in many churches in the present. A successor to the sanctus bell was the small bell hung in the belfry, formerly known as the 'priest's bell', or 'ting-tang', its purpose being to summon the priest, clerk or sexton and inform parishioners that the service was about to begin. A bell is still rung by a new incumbent during his installation service to indicate that he has authority of the parish.

'Turning the Devil's Stone' is part of a unique bell-ringing tradition at Shebbear, Devon. Every year, on the evening of 5 November, the bell-ringers sound a jangled peal on the church bells and then, armed with crowbars, the ringers and parishioners proceed to turn over a large stone in the churchyard known as the Devil's Boulder. According to local tradition it was accidentally dropped by Satan, or perhaps brought deliberately from nearby Henscott to stop them using it as a foundation for a new church. It is considered that misfortune would follow if this ritual was not steadfastly observed (Hole 1975: 101; Shuel 1985: 17, 19).

Another exclusive custom is the 'Lost in the Dark Peal' which takes place annually on 7 October at Twyford in Hampshire. In 1754, William Davis was riding on a dark night and became lost. He was saved from riding over a cliff by hearing the sound of Twyford's church bells and in gratitude, he bequeathed a pound for a peal of bells to be rung annually, followed by a feast for the bell ringers. The custom continues even though funds have long since run out.

For bells rung during the festivals of the church year and those tolled at funerals see Chapters 6 and 9 respectively.

The secular uses of church bells

Church bells were used extensively for secular reasons and in most churches there was a bell employed solely for this purpose, known as the 'common bell' (Camp 1988: 71). Even on Sundays, bells were tolled as domestic signals to local households. The bell that gave notice of an evening service, by virtue of its timing (which was usually at 12 noon), eventually became known as the 'potato bell', and became widely understood as a notice to cooks and housewives to begin food preparations. The 'pudding bell' was sounded in Warwickshire and other areas to show that it was time for the hot puddings to be cooled (Palmer 1976: 37) or to commence final dinner preparations. In certain parishes in Buckinghamshire and elsewhere, there was also a 'dinner' or 'oven bell' to advise villagers they could bring dough to be baked at the local manor-house (Cocks 1894: 279; Camp 1988: 72). On Shrove Tuesday, the 'pancake bell' was rung. It was originally known as the 'shriving bell' and was a summons to the faithful to be 'shriven' before the solemnity of Lent began. In some areas the bell was heard as a rhythmic message: 'Pan on, pan on' or 'The pan's a-burning, the pan's a-burning', depending on the ringing pattern. The custom of ringing the 'shriving bell' on Shrove Tuesday still happens at Burgh-le-Marsh Church, Lincolnshire.

Perhaps the earliest secular bell custom was the ringing of the *couvre-feu* or 'curfew bell' which may date from pre-Norman times (Camp 1988: 20). It became customary to warn people to put out their lights at 8.00 p.m. and to rest. This bell-ringing custom continued in some parishes into the twentieth century, long after the original usage had been abandoned. In agricultural communities the audible power of church bells made them effective as time-markers and to signal the start and finish of a day in the fields. The 'harvest bell' was rung at daybreak and at sunset. In nineteenth century England, cottagers had a legal right to gather leftovers after the harvest and the sexton would ring the 'gleaning bell' at 8.00 a.m. and again at 7.00 p.m. to tell the gleaners when to begin and end work (Cowrie 1996: 130). There were many local variants of these ringing customs performed to signal the start of seeding and crop-gathering (Baker 1974: 165). A 'morning bell' was also rung in many places to summon people to work. Bells were also regularly pealed to give public notice of any great civic or national celebrations or to warn of dangers such as fire.

In previous centuries, the countryside would have been a cacophony of sound at various times of the day, especially on Sundays and festival days. It was during the Reformation that moves were made to check the superstitious use and excessive ringing of bells and to simplify and regulate their use. However, a remarkable variety of customary peals continued to the end of the nineteenth century and bell-ringing still remains popular today.

Church bell superstitions

In popular religion, church bells had considerable presence to the extent that they were all-but personified by the community. Indeed up to the sixteenth century it was common practice to baptise and name them. Many bells carry inscribed rhymes, further suggesting that they are self-aware of their responsibility to communicate to the parish. Tenor bells around the country often display a sobering sentiment similar to the following example dating from 1745, at Amersham, Buckinghamshire:

> Unto the church I do you call
> Death to the grave will summon all.

(Camp 1988: 36)

Bells were believed to be invested with considerable supernatural powers capable of protecting the church and driving away evil spirits (Aubrey 1686: 22). There is a belief dating from the fifteenth century that bells could be rung to quell thunderstorms and lightning. A record exists of this occurring as late as 1870 at Dawlish, Devon (Camp 1988: 88). The mournful sound of bells has predictably inspired a number of omens. For instance, in Shropshire the church bell tolling with a heavy sound foretold a death (Burne 1883: 296) and a town clock striking while the church bells are ringing could presage a fire (Simpson and Roud 2000: 71). Folk medicine also benefited from the sonorous power of church bells. In the late Middle Ages, ringing was considered to have been effective during outbreaks of plague and pestilence, by dispelling the corrupt airs that were then believed to cause disease. They were also sometimes rung to help women in labour (Radford and Radford 1961: 43). However, the most widespread and well-documented belief asserts that the grease from the church bells, variously called 'bletch', 'dowment' or 'bell-comb', could be used as an ointment to cure shingles and ringworm (*Notes and Queries* [1907] 7: 206).

God's acre

The churchyard as a public space

We have seen that the church porch was essentially a public domain, so by extension, the churchyard – or 'God's acre', as it was colloquially known – was also a public space and largely unregulated territory. During the early medieval period, the flora of the churchyard belonged to the incumbent and he was responsible cutting the grass or grazing it with sheep (Dymond 1999: 469). Subsequently, it was not unusual for animals such as pigs, cows or even a parish bull to be allowed to freely graze there. The churchyard was also an arena for communicating parish news. It was common practice up to the beginning of the nineteenth century for the parish clerk in country districts to mount a grave stone on a Sunday morning and to announce to worshippers details of coming auction sales, particulars of rewards offered for the conviction of local felons, and notice of all kinds of parochial matters (Andrews 1891: 92). Many seasonal events and fund-raising entertainments also took place in the churchyard (see Chapter 5).

Some unusual local customs occurred in the churchyard before and after Sunday services. So for example, in the fourteenth century, it was a tradition in Lincolnshire for barbers to come and shave the parishioners in the churchyards on Easter Day and at other high festivals, before Matins. This was possibly symbolic of spiritual renewal (Wright and Lones 1940 Vol 1: 99). In a more playful spirit, at Northmere, Oxfordshire, after Evensong it was customary up to the mid-eighteenth century for men and women to throw large quantities of apples in the churchyard and those that were married that year threw three times as many at the rest; afterwards all involved were treated to bread, cheese and ale by the vicar (Hearne 1857: 552). Churchyards could also be legitimately used for darker purposes and during the Civil War (1642–51) military executions took place on the north side at Wootten Wawen, Kenilworth, and Stratford, Warwickshire (Palmer 1976: 36). This part of the churchyard may have been favoured because of its usual reservation for the burial of criminals and paupers.

Graves and popular belief

The consecrated ground surrounding a church has been used as a burial site for centuries. It became a place that inspired feelings of awe and where supernatural powers have been thought to be at their most intense. These emotions are informed by what Ron Hutton calls 'the numinous power of the dead' (Hutton 1994: 188). In pre-modern times, graves were treated with both caution and reverence, not so much out of respect for the deceased occupant but because of the wealth of positive and negative superstitious practices associated with them. In North Yorkshire, for example, to stand at the edge of an open grave was believed to cure a weak bladder (Blakeborough 1898: 145–6). Conversely, graves left open in Somerset, for example, were a bad omen and believed to eventually receive the corpse of the man who dug it (Tongue 1962: 107). However, the physical material of the churchyard, such as grass, soil or bones was considered most valuable in magical healing rites, suggesting that the presence of the dead and the soil in which their bodies were laid 'had some sort of contagious ameliorative power' (Tarlow 2011: 161). Before sanitary measures were imposed, corpses were laid in shallow graves. Rooting animals such as pigs and wild dogs routinely foraged in the churchyard so it was relatively easy to find bones and coffin parts lying near the surface.

Numerous cures were sought from graveyard material and artefacts. For example, moss growing on headstones was credited with medicinal powers, especially for the ailments of animals (Radford and Radford 1961:174). Coffin parts were especially sought after. In the medieval period, cramp was a persistent affliction and some people kept pieces of old coffin in their

Clypping the Church at Painswick, Gloucestershire. Photograph by churchwardens of Painswick church.

pockets as a preventative measure (Hone 1838: 253). 'Cramp rings' made from coffin hinges were also worn as a charm, while in northern England, the handles were preferred (Grose 1787: 55; Brockett 1846: Vol 1 111). Finger rings made from a lead coffin taken from a churchyard could also be worn for the same purpose (Robinson 1855: 35). Tombstones were popular sources of curative material and the defacement of many alabaster tombs is largely explained by the belief that scrapings taken from them and dissolved in vinegar or mixed with other ingredients were believed to have healing properties (Baker 1974: 166). This suggests that a certain basic chemical knowledge was being used alongside magical belief.

Complex folk rituals which involved running or crawling around a tomb in a particular direction a stated number of times were believed to have divinatory results or they could evoke magical powers for good or evil. So for example, at St Nicholas's churchyard in Stevenage, running twelve times around the tombstone to the left of the belfry door would bring out the Devil (Jones-Baker 1977:79). Some versions were practised as cures for a variety of ailments. In Launceston in Cornwall, for example, it was believed that a swelling on the neck could be cured by going before sunrise on 1 May to the

Church Clypping at Rode near Bath. Drawing by W.W. Wheatley, 1848.

grave of the last young person of the same gender to be interred in the churchyard; dew was to be gathered by passing the hand three times from the head to the foot of the grave to the affected part (Black 1883: 95–6). The measured stages of these rituals seem to imply that their complexity was somehow related to their success as a cure and combinations of three passes would suggest that the Holy Trinity is being invoked.

Church Clypping and Thread the Needle

One of the most colourful devotional customs to take place in a churchyard is 'clypping the church', which focuses entirely on affection and commitment to the church itself. The word 'clypping' is Anglo-Saxon in origin, and is derived from the word 'clyp-pan', meaning to 'embrace' or 'clasp' (Jones 1859: 244). The ceremony is traditionally held on Easter Monday or Shrove Tuesday and primarily involved children although in its later development, the whole church congregation might be involved; they would join together around the church exterior by holding hands in a ring, facing inwards. Once the circle had formed, they would be cheered on by onlookers and sometimes a 'clypping hymn' would be sung. The clypping custom was in many areas often preceded by the game known as 'Thread the Needle', in which two children hold up their arms to form an arch, while others in line run or creep underneath (Partridge 1912: 196–203). Dancing was also an accompaniment in some parishes and all of these activities were clearly intended to heighten the sense of joy with parishioners expressing their love for the church by literally embracing the building and the surrounding people. The ceremony would usually conclude with a sermon delivered in the church, followed by refreshments.

Many churches formerly celebrated the clypping custom although St Mary's church at Painswick, Gloucestershire, is still the most notable exponent of the ceremony; the tradition was revived there in the nineteenth century. A particular feature of the Painswick custom included the serving of 'Puppy Dog Pie' which used to be given out after the service. Despite speculation

The lych-gate at Sampford Courtenay, Devon, showing the coffin rest just inside the gates. Photograph by Bob Trubshaw.

that local dogs were originally consigned to the cooking pot, the puppies were actually made of china!

The clypping ceremony was also kept up with particular enthusiasm in the nineteenth century at Cradley, Worcestershire, and also at Birmingham where children would clip St Martin's Church near the Bull Ring and afterwards proceed to St Phillip's Cathedral where the ceremony was repeated (Palmer 1976:158). During the last century there have been a few revivals of this ceremony and venues include St Peter's Church in Tankersley, Yorkshire, St Mary the Virgin, Wirksworth, Derbyshire, St Laurence, Upwey, Dorset, and St. Peter's Edgmond, Shropshire. Customs of a very similar character and possibly serving the same purpose, were also observed at Wellington in Shropshire and Beckington, Somerset, in the nineteenth century. On Shrove Tuesday children met in the churchyard to blow trumpets. They all joined hands and formed a ring round the outside of the church, and the trumpets were blown again (Vaux 1894: 228). For other churchyard dancing customs and festivities – see chapter 4.

The lychgate

The entrance to a churchyard was a simple affair until lychgates were invented after 1552, when the *Book of Common Prayer* required all funeral services to take place out in the churchyard. The lych-gate (Old English *lic*, meaning 'corpse') or 'corpse-gate' is characterised by a gabled roof, and it was here that the priest met the corpse while part of the service was read before burial. It also served to shelter the bereaved and the pall-bearers while the bier was brought from the church. Some lych-gates were provided with large flat 'lich-stones' upon which the corpse was laid.

Superstition was quick to embrace the lych-gate and the 'churchyard watcher' was believed to reside there; this was the spirit of the last person to have been buried in the precincts, who held this office until another was buried therein.

A unique church gate ritual is the bidding for grazing rights at Wishford Magna church, near Salisbury, Wiltshire. This is believed to date from the sixteenth century, and is an auction for the grazing rights on two pieces of land, Bonhams Mead and Abbey Mead, from 1 November until 12 August. The bidding starts at 8.00 p.m. at the church gates and finishes at sunset; the key of the church door is used by the churchwarden as a gavel . The service is locally known by the misnomer of the Midsummer Tithes (Day 1999: 70). For other customs concerning churchyard gates see Chapters 8 and 9.

Chapter Four

The Commemorating Church

The Church has always placed commemoration and the blessing of good works at the heart of its worshipping life. The seasonal holy days remember essential moments in the life of Christ, and the Eucharist which is the most central act of worship, is in itself an act of commemoration and thanksgiving. We have seen in Chapter 1 that the celebration of the canonised saints was integral to the unfolding liturgical year, although only a few of these saints are ritually commemorated in the Church of England today. Special services of remembrance continue to be held for war heroes and others who have given their lives for their country or community. However, self-commemoration is also a very human desire and affluent parishioners of the past could take decisive steps to be remembered in perpetuity. By making bequests or endowments for special rites they were able to ensure a continual association with the gratitude, prayer and worshipping life of the Church.

In the fourteenth century, for example, it became customary for a wealthy testator to leave gifts of vestments, books and lights in his will as tangible ways to perpetuate his former life. For the wealthy however, the primary means of ensuring lasting memorial was through the establishment of a 'chantry' (French *chanter*, from Latin *cantare*, meaning 'to sing'). This was a fund established to pay for a priest to celebrate sung masses, generally for the soul of the deceased donor and frequently with the inclusion of alms for the poor. Chantry chapels were either built on private land or within the parish church, where a dedicated chantry priest would have been charged to perform these functions. Chantries were condemned and dissolved during the Reformation, but acts of self-commemoration continued to persist in other forms. Some were undoubtedly provided less from compassion than to give spiritual benefits to the donor. These legacies included annual sermons, parish doles of food, drink and money, or other charitable actions. There has always been a concern to try and honour the wishes of a dying person and to make sure that they are legally enforced so far as is socially acceptable (Thomas 1997: 602). As a result, an extraordinary range of local customs and public charities still persist, reminding us that there is always an enduring relationship between the living and the dead. Financial legacies to provide some measure of support for the poor were extremely common but many of these have faded away, either because the funds have dwindled or because the terms of a bequest are no longer relevant in the modern world.

Remembering the saints today

Most of the saints no longer have a national celebration, but are commemorated locally at patronal festivals, although all of the recognised saints are, at the very least, remembered in prayers of thanksgiving on their appointed days. The most celebrated saint in modern England is St George who is remembered on 23 April. In many parish churches, equestrian statues of St George were erected and solemn ceremonies held in his honour. At St Paul's Cathedral, London, the Order of St Michael and St George hold an annual service. Members wear traditional scarlet-tinted blue mantles at a ceremony to commemorate deceased members of the Order and to install new members. A similar service occurs in St George's Chapel, Windsor, which Edward III dedicated to the saint in 1348. On the Sunday nearest 23 April, scouts and guides throughout England parade through towns and attend a special St George's Day service at their local church. In recent years there have been attempts to recover the national importance of St George and bells are now rung in some parishes on 23 April while St George's flag is flown from the top of every English church tower. Similarly, St David, the sixth century patron saint of Wales is honoured on 1 March throughout England and Wales with special services and processions.

St Alban died at the hands of the Romans in 303 and is honoured as the first Christian martyr. His feast day is 22 June and his martyrdom was formerly celebrated at St Alban's Cathedral with a rose festival. In memory of a legendary incident in the saint's life, local school children gathered roses and carried them in procession to St Alban's shrine. Later, women made the flowers into a solid carpet which remained in the chapel throughout the week (Spicer 1954: 85). St Alban is now celebrated with a 'pilgrimage' from Roman Verulanium which re-enacts his last steps and ends with his execution outside the Cathedral. (see photographs overleaf). A similar celebration takes place at Ripon Cathedral which is dedicated to St Wilfrid, the seventh century bishop of Ripon. Every year on the Saturday before the first Monday in August, he is celebrated with a parade which is led by an

Left and opposite: *The St Albans Pilgrimage, St Albans Cathedral, Hertfordshire. Photographs by Arun Kataria.*

actor playing the saint on horseback. The Dean meets the 'saint' at the west door of the cathedral where a service of thanksgiving takes place.

A saint who is widely honoured in the world of music is St Cecilia who is patron saint of musicians. Her feast day is 22 November and, since 1946 on the Wednesday nearest to this day, a festival service has been held in London. The service rotates between St Paul's Cathedral, Westminster Abbey and Westminster Cathedral. The music is sung by the combined choirs of the three churches and every year a new anthem is specially commissioned for the event. The service also features a spectacular robed procession by the City Livery Companies. St Blaise is uniquely celebrated on his feast day (3 February) at the Roman Catholic church of St Etheldreda in London because of his intercessory power to heal throat diseases. During the service two candles are consecrated, crossed and held over the heads or against the throats of the afflicted people being blessed. This ceremony is not performed in the Church of England although the feast day is observed in many parishes of the Anglican Communion but only as a commemoration.

Many saints' days were characterised by open air entertainments and processions rather than acts of devotion. St Bartholomew's Day (24 August) still has an element of fun associated with it. At Sandwich, Kent, the day is celebrated with a special service in the chapel of the Hospital of St Bartholomew, followed by a race for local children who are given currant buns. Perhaps the custom originated in the twelfth century, when free food was distributed to the Canterbury pilgrims (Spicer 1954: 113). St Edmund, who was recently adopted as Patron Saint of Suffolk, is also celebrated with a bun dole on his feast day (20 November) at the local church in Southwold, Suffolk. Sticky buns are given to local primary school children in memory of the saints' martyrdom. Children also have a significant role in the commemoration of the sixth century Welsh hermit, St Nectan at Hartland, Devon, on 17 June. According to legend, on his arrival from Wales he was attacked by robbers and beheaded. The saint promptly picked up his head and continued on his journey, but wherever a drop of blood hit the ground a foxglove sprang up. Traditionally the event is commemorated with a special service followed by a procession in which children carry foxgloves.

The Thorn Cutting Ceremony, at St John the Baptist Church, Glastonbury, Somerset is a unique custom which has evolved from the story of a saint. The famous Glastonbury Thorn is a type of hawthorn that flowers at Christmas and is believed by some to have originated from the Middle East. Reputedly, St Joseph of Arimathea visited England nearly two thousand years ago and visited the Isle of Avalon, Glastonbury. He was carrying a staff which he thrust into the ground. This was believed to have taken root, eventually growing into a tree. The original tree was cut down by Cromwell's soldiers in the Civil War but trees found across the country are said to have been grown from cuttings, such as at Appleton, Cheshire. On the second Wednesday in December, a piece of the thorn is cut, then blessed at the altar and sent to the Queen.

Commemorative customs in the City of London

The City of London, with its love of pageantry and colourful ritual, has continued to maintain some intriguing commemorative church customs. Sir John Cass was an important benefactor in the East End of London and he is remembered as founder of the school to which gave his name. Sir John intended to leave all his property to the school but because of his poor health, he struggled to write his will. According to tradition, he managed to sign the document but suddenly suffered a fatal haemorrhage that stained the writing quill with his blood. On or near 20 February a commemorative service is held at the Church of St Botolph-without-Aldgate. The event commences with a procession of around thirty children from the Sir John Cass Primary school together with guests. The service includes performances by pupils from both the primary and secondary schools supported by the Sir John Cass Foundation. The children and staff all wear red feathers, which appear on the Cass coat of arms, as a token of homage to the school's founder. The day is sometimes known as 'Red Feather Day'.

Another act of remembrance involving a feather is the quaint ceremony of Changing John Stow's Quill, which is held annually at St Andrew's Undershaft annually, on or near 5 April. This little ritual remembers historian John Stow, who was a loyal member of the church congregation but best known for writing *The Survey of London* in 1598. The ceremony commences with a prominent historian addressing the congregation who then process to the Stow monument. He then removes the old quill and passes a new one to the Lord Mayor who then places it in Stow's hand.

Not all commemorative rituals have a positive meaning associated with them. The Knollys Rose Ceremony which takes place at All Hallows-by-the-Tower certainly has a penitential quality about it. A freshly-plucked rose is presented to the Lord Mayor at the Mansion House by the churchwardens. This is given in commemoration of Sir Robert Knollys who was fined in 1381 for building a footbridge between his two houses, across Seething Lane in the City of London without planning permission. The church stands on the site of one of Knolly's houses.

Changing John Stow's Quill, St Andrew's Undershaft. Photograph by Mike Paterson of London Histortians.

Anniversary commemorations

Throughout the Church year there are many other imaginative and nostalgic acts of commemoration honouring famous people on the anniversary of their death. London churches observe memorial services to honour Charles I on 30 January, the anniversary of his execution in 1649. Special prayers are offered and a wreath-laying ceremony takes place at his statue outside the Banqueting Hall in London, which was the site of his beheading. Afterwards, a High Mass takes place inside the Banqueting House where relics of the Charles I are placed on the altar and venerated. Further commemorations of the King include a procession of choristers from St Martin-in-the-Fields to Trafalgar Square and a memorial service at St George's Chapel, Windsor Castle. Samuel Pepys the diarist is similarly commemorated at a service at St Olave's Church, Hart Street in London on or near 26 May and the Lord Mayor places a laurel wreath in front of his memorial. Katharine of Aragon, the first wife of Henry VIII, was buried at Peterborough Cathedral following her death in 1536; and is remembered during an annual festival in late January, which includes a special memorial service and a Roman Catholic Mass.

A unique commemoration of a royal individual is the celebration at the Church of the Holy Cross, Avening, Gloucestershire, which is known locally as 'Pig-Face Day'. The feast commemorates Queen Matilda, wife of William the Conqueror, who consecrated the church in 1080. This is the only service to commemorate the commissioning of a church by a Queen of England. The Queen was spurned by a lover called Brittic and had him thrown into prison where he died. She was overcome with remorse and as an act of penance, commissioned a church to be built at Avening. When the church was completed the builders had a feast of boar's head. After evensong on every second year on the Sunday after Holy Cross Day (14 September), parishioners are served with sandwiches containing meat from a wild boar which is followed by fruit.

The most moving services are those given for people who have given great help to humanity. Florence Nightingale, known as the 'Lady of the Lamp', performed an extraordinary selfless duty to sick and wounded soldiers. She is commemorated annually at Westminster Abbey on a day nearest to her date of birth on 12 May. The nursing services and the ideals and standards she promoted are also celebrated. A lamp of traditional design is carried by nurses in procession from St George's Chapel to the Dean of Westminster who places it on the High Altar (Brentnall 1975: 180–1).

Humanity has also been served well by comedy, and the world of clowning is also celebrated at a unique memorial service which is held for the celebrated English clown Joseph Grimaldi, who died in 1837. This event takes place at Holy Trinity Church in Dalston, East London, every first Sunday in February. This has been an annual tradition since 1946 when a group of Christian clowns met informally. In 1967 the clowns were given permission to attend in their costumes. Hundreds of clowns flock to this event from all over the world in full attire, and the service is followed by a show for the children. A wreath is also laid on Grimaldi's memorial.

Remembering loss of life

The most poignant act of remembrance in the English calendar is Remembrance Sunday, held on the second Sunday in November, which is the Sunday nearest to 11 November, Armistice Day. This is the anniversary of the ending of the hostilities of the First World War at 11.00 a.m. in 1918. Paper poppies are sold in aid of ex-servicemen, because the common poppy grew in such abundance around the trenches of Flanders. The two-minute period of silence at 11.00 a.m. is maintained as a sign of respect for sixty million people who died in the war. The parade in London of serving soldiers and veterans is an event of national significance although most parish churches have their own services in which wreaths are placed at war memorials on village greens or in churchyards. Other Remembrance

The Clown's Service, Holy Trinity Church, Dalston, London. Photograph by Doc Rowe. See also the frontispiece.

observances include the Dunkirk Veterans' Services although they have become less frequent as these ex-servicemen are now dwindling in numbers. A unique commemoration is the annual Cyclists Memorial Service which takes place on a Sunday in May on Meriden Green, in Warwickshire. This event has been held since 1921 in memory of cyclists who gave their lives in conflicts around the world.

Some of the great historical battles fought in defence of England are also remembered by the Church. For example, the Battle of Townton, one of the bloodiest conflicts in the War of the Roses which took place on Palm Sunday 1461 is annually re-enacted and remembered with a moving open-air service. The Battle of Tewkesbury of 1471 is also recalled with a re-enactment of the storming of the Abbey concluding with a service of Compline. The Battle of Trafalgar which saw a historic victory of the British Navy over the French and Spanish in 1805 is commemorated on 21 October; wreaths are laid at the tomb of Admiral Lord Nelson at St Paul's Cathedral and on board *HMS Victory* at Portsmouth. The historic signal 'England expects that every man will do his duty', is sent from the ship at 8 a.m. and a memorial service is held on board. The Battle of Nevilles' Cross in 1346 is commemorated annually on 29 May or the nearest Saturday from the top of Durham Cathedral tower (see Chapter 6).

In a completely different vein, but no less significant is the annual outdoor service that takes place annually at Eyam in Derbyshire on the last Sunday in August, in memory of the many plague victims who died there in 1665. People had quickly become contaminated with the disease after handling infected cloth from London. The rector, Rev William Mompesson, attempted to seal off the village to halt the spread of the virus to the rest of the county. The local villages responded with kindness by leaving food on the boundary stones and coins were left in a water trough into which vinegar had been poured to sterilise them. Nowadays a procession forms at the church of St Lawrence and passes some of the surviving plague cottages on its way to Cucklet Dell, where the service takes place (Day 1999: 125). The tomb of Mompesson's wife, Catherine, who was buried next to her husband, is in the churchyard and every year it is decorated with a rose wreath on 'Plague Sunday' (Hole 1978: 235–6).

Individual memorial bequests

The determination for an individual to be remembered in perpetuity has provided a legacy of enduring bequests, charities and endowments in the literature of church lore. Food and drink doles were extremely common and many annuities provided for simple acts such the tolling of 'early rising' or curfew bells, the dressing of graves with flowers or planting trees in the churchyard. However, a substantial number of these legacies were blatant attempts to ensure that the communal memory of the deceased was renewed. For example, requests for candles and torches to be burned on the anniversary of a death were common up to the nineteenth century, but occasionally these could be taken to extremes. At Swaffham, Norfolk, for example, one Simon Blake appointed 'a lamp to burn by his grave on all holidays and Lord's days, from Matins to Compline, and the bellman of the town of Swaffham to take care of it' (Gasquet 1906: 119). Perhaps less demanding were the annual musical commemorations such as singing psalms or anthems. One of the best known in this tradition is that of William Hubbard, who in his will of 1774, left one guinea to establish the custom of singing hymns over his grave at St Mary-in-Arden church, Market Harborough, Leicestershire. This unbroken tradition still takes place every Easter Saturday at 6.00 p.m. even though the church is now in ruins. The custom of singing from the tower of St Magdelens College, Oxford is discussed in Chapter 6.

Henry Travice of Leigh, Greater Manchester, attempted to keep his memory alive by quieter means. He stipulated in his will of 1627 that forty people had to pass over his grave which is located under the floor of the church. In return for this curious request he left the sum of ten pounds to be divided by the local vicars amongst the parishes of Leigh, Atherton and Tyseley. The

Singing at the grave of William Hubbard, St Mary-in-Arden, Market Harborough. Photograph by Brian Shuel.

ceremony still continues but the number of participants has diminished significantly in recent years and now only three people cross his grave after the Maundy Thursday evening service. William Glanville, however, went even further in ensuring his communal remembrance. Under the terms of his will of 1717, five poor boys under the age of sixteen who qualified for forty shillings each had to stand with their right hands resting on his tomb in Wotton churchyard near Dorking, Surrey. While holding this pose they were expected to recite the Lord's Prayer, the Apostle's Creed and the Ten Commandments. Furthermore they were expected to read aloud Chapter 15 of the first Letter of Corinthians and write two verses from the same passage in clear legible writing. This annual test took place in early February but bad weather often meant that it was rescheduled to a date near Ascension Day (Christian 1966: 94).

Possibly the loudest and most eccentric commemorative custom is the Firing of the Fenny Poppers, which takes place on St Martin's Day (11 November). This is the patronal festival of the church of St Martin, Fenny Stratford near Bletchley, Buckinghamshire. The Fenny Poppers are six tankard-shaped miniature cannon which are fired annually on 11 November in memory of Dr Thomas Willis, the founder of the science of neurology, who died on this date. He was the grandfather of a local eccentric, Browne Willis who built

Left: *Charging the Fenny Poppers, St Martin's, Fenny Stratford, Buckinghamshire.*

Right: *Firing the Fenny Poppers.*

Photographs by Doc Rowe.

St Martin's Church in Fenny Stratford and he is believed to have started the custom in 1740. Each popper is ignited from a long poker heated in a brazier and traditionally the first is lit by the incumbent of St Martin's Church. The event originally took place in the churchyard but because of damage to buildings it has in recent years moved to a local sports field. The reason for introducing the miniature cannons is uncertain but clearly reflects the eccentricity of its founder (Legg 2001).

Financial bequests

The greatest benefits to a community were endowments providing some monetary support to the church or poor parishioners. Many of these legacies were humble pragmatic gifts of articles such as food, clothing, gloves or shoes for the poor of the parish. Others reflected the particular philanthropic obsessions of the benefactor and sometimes have a distinctly idiosyncratic flavour. Typical examples from the early nineteenth century include provision for keeping boys quiet in church at Wolverhampton, Staffordshire, taking care of the parson's horse at Yapham-cum-Meltonby, Yorkshire, while he was on duty, or the purchase of a parish cow at Bebington, Cheshire. Bell-ringing endowments were common, such as the tolling of a bell at Woodstock, Oxfordshire, to guide travellers at night or an 'early rising bell' at

Huntingdon. Other widespread legacies were intended to encourage prayer and the development of religious knowledge, or promote marriage in the community.

Some bequests demonstrated remarkable audacity, such as the endowment at All Saints Church, Newmarket, Suffolk still surviving at the beginning of the nineteenth century which offered twenty pounds to a man if he married a young woman from the church on Maundy Thursday. If the money was not claimed in a given year, then it would by default go to a horse-racing fund! (Edwards 1842: 57, 68, 99–100, 201, 190, 221–2). The element of monetary distribution in many of these charities was often abandoned in later years because, as the interest accrued from the original bequest began to diminish, so the purchasing power of the money also decreased.

Certain bequests were intended to be fulfilled immediately on the death of the deceased. One Thomas Tuke of Wath, Yorkshire, who died in 1810, bequeathed a penny to every child who should be present at his funeral. As a result the churchyard walks were literally lined with up to seven hundred children and pennies were duly distributed to them. He also ordered forty dozen penny buns to be thrown from the church tower at noon every Christmas Day, leaving a sum of money for the purpose. For some years the buns were distributed in accordance with the will but eventually, owing to the disruptive behaviour that ensued, only six dozen were thrown from the tower and the remainder were quietly given away below (Vaux 1894: 139–40).

Dicing for Bibles, All Saint's Church, St Ives, Cambridgeshire. Photograph by Fr Mark Amey .

A monetary dole still takes place annually at the Church of St Mary the Virgin at Hartfield in East Sussex on Good Friday, when money is given to the poor of the parish. The distribution originated in the seventeenth century when Nicholas Smith bequeathed a sum of money and the interest was to be used to fund the charity. According to local legend, Smith travelled around disguised as a beggar to see how he was treated; Hartfield was the only place which offered him a warm welcome so he elected to be buried there. Poor widows were the frequent recipients of monetary doles and one of the most famous distributions is the giving of the Widows' Sixpence at St Bartholomew the Great, London. In the past this was a charity dole of money and food given to widows of the parish of St Bartholomew the Great at Smithfield in London, but now hot cross buns are distributed to anyone who attends the morning service on Good Friday. The origins of the custom are lost, but Joshua Butterworth gave funds, and his name, to the event in the late nineteenth century. A similar charity still takes place at St Leonard's Church, Keevil in Wiltshire on the first or second Sunday Family service after Easter which resulted from the bequest of a local farmer, George Taylor in his will of 1852 to provide buns for local children.

Some testators could be very uncompromising about their intended recipients. William Underhill of Eldersfield, Herefordshire, left money in 1647 to the 'honest poor, not bastards nor any known dishonest poor'. The vicar called the names of the chosen, who received the money from the churchwarden while the latter was sitting on a chair at the head of Underhill's tomb. A least one charity generated sufficient funds to allow a weekly distribution, so at 4.00 p.m. every Saturday at Wiveton Church, Norfolk, the 'charity bell' was tolled and twelve elderly villagers received money as 'pensions' in a blue bag. This provision came from the will of Ralph Greenaway, a wealthy merchant, dated 1558 (Christian 1966: 15).

Inspecting Mary Gibsons Tomb, St Nicholas' Church, Sutton, Surrey. Photograph by Brian Shuel.

Some charities could be quite bold and self-indulgent. The so-called 'Pretty Maids' Charity' for instance, was instituted in 1841 by Rev Thomas Merrick, brother of the rector of Holsworthy, Devon. He left money to be invested in government stock, the interest to be given annually to the most worthy, quiet, handsome, single woman who was under thirty years of age and attended church regularly. The one chosen was concealed in Holsworthy parish church until noon, when she emerged from the tower door (Kightly 1986: 190–1). However, the most controversial church legacy must be that of Rev Dr Robert Wilde at All Saints Church, St Ives, Cambridgeshire. When he died in 1679, he made provision in his will for a bequest of money to provide a dozen bibles, six for the boys and six for girls, to be won annually by casting dice on the altar. Wilde was known for his zealous Puritan outlook and wished to demonstrate that God's word was in the bible and not in liturgical show and spectacle. The use of the altar for gambling purposes inevitably offended the sensibilities of parishioners although the dicing ceremony still takes place every Whit Tuesday since 1880 on a small table in the church (Roud 2006: 271).

Another curious and longstanding attempt to defy the ravages of time is the legacy of a wealthy widow named Mary Gibson who is interred at

St Nicholas' Church, Sutton in Surrey. She died on 12 August 1793 and, under the terms of her will, a sermon was to be preached on the anniversary of her death – but with conditions attached. Gibson made a considerable bequest to Christ's Hospital School, but in return, the school's governors were required to carefully inspect the Gibson family vault beneath the church on the day, and ensure that any necessary repairs were carried out. A fear of being buried alive may have been at the heart of the original bequest, although it is unclear what those undertaking the inspection of the tomb in later years were expected to find. The churchwardens continued to undertake this duty, but the opening of the tomb has now been discontinued.

Bread doles and charities

Food charities and bequests have taken many forms including biscuits, currant buns, fish, meat, wheat, cakes and plum pudding, often in association with wine or ale. Bread has probably been the commonest item in charitable distributions. Christmas was a very popular season for food doles. For example, at Piddlehinton, Dorset, there was a festive distribution of mince pies, ale and bread to more than three hundred people and at Great Barr in Staffordshire, the rector gave to all comers on Christmas Day, as much bread, beef, vinegar and mustard as they could eat (Tate 1946: 114). Easter was also a popular time for food doles and a few also dared to ease the austerity of Lent. Some of these offerings have also been bound up with distributions of money. The dispensing of food as dole had mixed motives and provided a socially acceptable way for the wealthy classes to display their power and to reinforce class divisions within the community (Black 1981: 59). Some food doles, however, have been exceptionally generous. For example, the only daily distribution which still continues is at Cartmel Priory, Cumbria. Bread is stored at the church to be given to any poor person who may request it on any day of the week, in accordance with the will of Rowland Briggs of Swallowmire, who perished in the great storm of 1703 and left money for this purpose (Stockdale 1872: 164).

The bun distribution at St Bartholomew's Church, London, has already been mentioned but another similar charity dole also took place at St Michael's Church, Bristol. Large fruit buns called 'tuppenny starvers' were given out every Easter Tuesday at the church. The church has now closed, so the event is held privately at the local school where it has evolved into a Bun Festival. The origin of this custom dates back to the days when the poor could afford only black bread and this special occasion gave them the opportunity of receiving at least one meal of white bread every year.

Some doles could be regarded as tokenistic, yielding more to boisterous entertainment than feeding the poor. The St Briavel's Bread and Cheese Dole

The Bread and Cheese Dole at St Mary's Church, St Briavel's, Herefordshire. Photograph by Doc Rowe.

seems to fall into this category. Every year on Whit Sunday at St Briavels, Herefordshire, crowds of local people congregate outside St Mary's church in the hope of catching pieces of bread and cheese which are thrown into the air from overflowing baskets. This distribution dates back to the twelfth century when dole claimers could be anyone who paid a penny to the Earl of Hereford who was then Lord of the Forest of Dean. This entitled them to gather wood from nearby woodlands (Hartland 1893–4).

Another charitable bread and cheese dole takes place at Biddenden, Kent, at Eastertide which dates back to the twelfth century. Special hard and almost inedible biscuits in the shape of the Chulkhurst twins are given out. According to a local legend Eliza and Mary Chulkhurst were Siamese twins who died within hours of each other; they left twenty acres of land still known as the Bread and Cheese Lands to the church to support a charitable dole which continues today, although the original motives are not entirely clear. The bread and cheese goes to those in need but anyone who attends the ceremony may receive a biscuit (Hole 1978: 35–36).

By contrast, there is a remarkable graveside dole that takes place at St Mary-the-Virgin, Braughing, near Bishop's Stortford, Hertfordshire. It originates with the will of Matthew Wall, a sixteenth century farmer whose coffin was being carried from his home to the churchyard, when the bearers suddenly

The Rector after blessing the Hallaton 'bottles' at the Butter Cross, Easter Monday 1999. The lady with the basket has just distributed 'penny loaves' (bread rolls). Photograph by Bob Trubshaw.

tripped on some dead leaves and dropped it. To the amazement of all present, he stepped out of the coffin, clearly revived by the sudden jolt. He died over twenty years later but in gratitude for being saved from a premature burial, he left a bequest for a small sum of money to be given to each of twenty children on 2 October. On this day, the church bells are still rung and the children sweep the route of the coffin to the church and prayers are said while Matthew Wall's grave is tended. Matthew lived to a good age and the day is locally known as 'Old Man's Day'.

Another legacy originally given in gratitude has resulted in one of the most high-spirited celebrations in England. This is the hare-pie scramble and bottle-kicking ceremony which takes place at St Michael and All Angels, Hallaton, Leicestershire on Easter Monday. A hare pie is paraded in a procession from the Fox Inn to the lych gate, where it is sliced, blessed by the Rector and 'distributed' to the local people – by flinging it in the air. About an hour later another procession is formed to where a bottle-kicking match commences between competing village teams. The 'bottles' are actually three painted wooden kegs, two of which contain beer. The custom seemingly began in 1770, when the Rector of Hallaton was given a piece of land, which according to local legend, was given in gratitude by two women

The Rector blessing the hare pie at the lych-gate, Hallaton on Easter Monday in 1999. Photograph by Bob Trubshaw.

who were saved after being chased by a bull! The original bequest required that two hare pies, two dozen loaves of bread and a quantity of ale be provided for the poor of the parish, which had to be scrambled for in public (Trubshaw 1990).

Cakes and ale doles

The distribution of Pax Cakes which takes place at Sellack at St Tysillio's Church, and St John the Baptist's church, Kings Caple (both in Herefordshire) is a dole with a very particular intention. It is a charity distribution and the round shortbread-like biscuits are given out by the vicar after the Sunday service on Palm Sunday. Each 'pax' (Latin for 'peace') cake is stamped with the image of the Paschal Lamb and offered with a blessing of 'Peace and good neighbourhood' which is spoken with each gift. The dole is believed to have originated with the 1570 bequest of a local landowner, Lady Scudamore, although there have been earlier attributions. Beer was originally part of the distribution and both the drink and cake were intended to be

Above and opposite: *Orange and Lemons Service, St Clement Danes, Strand, London. Photographs by Doc Rowe.*

consumed within the church. The donor believed that any quarrels could be dispelled and peace and good friendship established over a communal meal before taking Easter communion a week later (Hole 1978: 233–4). The custom was also formerly observed at Hentland in the same county.

The giving of cakes and ale also feature in the Jankyn Smith Charity which takes place on the Thursday following Plough Monday at Bury St Edmunds, Suffolk. Jankyn Smith was a significant benefactor to the town of Bury St Edmunds in Suffolk; under the terms of his will, a requiem mass for his soul was to be held each year at St Mary's church on the anniversary of his death in 1481, followed by a provision of food and drink at the Guildhall. The charity still continues and residents of the almshouses which he also founded are given money. This is the oldest endowed charity in the country known to be still in existence.

Cakes also feature in the Methodist 'Love Feasts' which are modelled on the 'Agape' (from the Greek word meaning 'love') feasts of the early Church, where the wealthy brought food for the poor. The most notable love feast is held in a large barn at Alport Castle in Derbyshire on the first Sunday of July; unaccompanied hymns are sung and each participant takes fruitcake and water to share as a commemoration of Methodist fellowship. A similar feast has taken place under a gospel elm at Wicken in Northamptonshire.

Only a few fruit doles have been recorded. The best known is the Oranges and Lemons Service for children at St Clement Danes, Strand, London in March. During the service, the 'oranges and lemons' rhyme is read and the fruit is distributed outside. This is believed to be a legacy of the days when barges bringing cargoes of citrus fruits from ships moored down-river were unloaded on the shore of the Thames just south of the church (Brentnall 1975: 171). Another orange distribution is made at St Mary's Church, Sileby, Leicestershire on a Sunday in May. The origin and meaning of this custom is uncertain but may relate to a commemoration of the victory at Waterloo in 1815 (Kightly 1986: 177). A distribution of apples takes place at Ripon Cathedral on Christmas Day – See Chapter 6.

Annual sermons

A popular form of individual endowment was in the form of a thematic annual sermon and numerous examples are found in parish records. The commemorative sermon is an essentially Protestant phenomenon for the purpose of providing an annual injection of spiritual instruction. Some of these are still honoured today. A notably survival is the 'Handy Sermon', preached at St Giles's, Oxford, on or about 10 March. This was founded under the terms of the 1622 will of William Handy who was presumably a zealous convert to the Reformed religion and wished his death to be commemorated with a sermon giving thanks to God for delivering the nation from 'Popery and Idolatry'.

A good number of endowed sermons were also accompanied by bread and bun doles, which may have been intended to ensure a more substantial congregation (Kightly 1996: 204:). The character of these sermons has sometimes been penitential or instructive, on a topic of particular interest to the donor. Others can be a form of heartfelt gratitude for surviving warfare or a life-threatening experience. At Newark, Nottinghamshire, for example, Hercules Clay left a provision for an annual sermon in gratitude that he and his family were saved from a fire that destroyed their home. It takes place on or about 11 March. George Dalton was saved from drowning and in his will of 1556, he left a thanksgiving legacy for a 'Rush Sermon' to be preached St Giles Church, Farnborough, Kent, which still takes place on the first Sunday after 29 June. The theme is the 'frailty of life' and the church porch is strewn with rushes as a thanksgiving (Ashley 1988: 187). The Lion Sermon, preached annually on 16 October at St Katharine Cree church, in the City of London, commemorates the 'wonderful escape' of a former Lord Mayor of London, Sir John Gayer, from a lion which he met in the desert whilst travelling the wilds of Turkey. Gayer allegedly recalled the story of Daniel in the Lions' Den (Daniel 6: 16–24), fell on his knees and prayed for deliverance (Hole 1978: 180).

Endowed sermons are particularly common in the City of London and the Spital Sermon is probably the oldest annual sermon still to be observed there. It dates from the lengthy addresses on the Resurrection given from an open-air pulpit in the churchyard of the twelfth century Priory Church of St Mary Spital in the area that is now Spitalfields. On the second Wednesday after Easter, the Lord Mayor of London, the Court of Common Council and Court of Aldermen and city dignitaries from the Guildhall walk in procession to St Lawrence Jewry church where the sermon is now preached.

Another notable observance is the 'Bubble Sermon' given to members of the London Stationers' Company at St Martin's-within-Ludgate. The company process to the church on the first Tuesday in June where they are annually reminded that 'Life is but a bubble'. This was a bequest in the will of Richard Johnson, who was an eighteenth century benefactor to the company. The capture of Guy Fawkes was a favourite Protestant theme of commemoration in many churches and typically, on 5 November or the nearest Sunday, the 'Gunpowder Plot Sermon', is preached at St Mary-Le-Bow, London.

Sermons on human morals

There have been many legacies for sermons on various aspects of questionable human behaviour. Annual sermons on the sin of pride are preached at Salisbury Cathedral and at St Aldates, Oxford – where it is a challenge for many because it is preached in Latin! The 1706 will of Michael Solomon left money for a sermon against drunkenness which is occasionally preached at St Wulfram's Church, Grantham (Kightly 1986: 205). The ethical concerns of genetic engineering seem to have been anticipated in the 'Vegetable Sermon' preached at Whitsun in St Giles', Cripplegate, London. This sermon recalls the work of Thomas Fairchild who successfully created the first hybridised plant in 1720, but died worrying that he had been 'playing God'; he endowed a sermon to be preached on the supreme role of God in the creation of different species.

Some obsolete sermons are worthy of note because they reflect the particular concerns of their time. So for instance, until 1812 a sixteenth century annuity was still being paid for an annual sermon at Huntingdon to be preached against belief in witchcraft. At Berrow, Worcestershire, Susannah Cocks Nanfan left a sum of money in 1775 for a sermon against duelling, after her lover had been killed in a duel with her brother (Noake 1868: 32). This was still taking place annually towards the end of the nineteenth century. However, the concept of the annual sermon has continued and some preaching bequests are of quite recent origin. For example, in 1947 at Crawley, Sussex, a sum of money was left for an annual sermon to be preached on kindness to animals and in the 1950s, a St George's Day sermon was founded at St Peter's, Nottingham.

Chapter Five

The Church in the Community

Here we explore processions, walks, perambulations, pilgrimages and other customs where churchgoers demonstrate their faith to the wider world. Many church traditions bring the faithful out into the larger community. The primary religious function of communal events is to make a public profession of faith, and these may be undertaken out of devotion, blessing or thanksgiving. Other activities may focus on raising money for the work of the Church and motivations might include the commemorative obligation of a legacy to affirm an allegiance, a commemoration or a celebration which helps to bond a community.

Rogationtide processions

Processions are a natural form of public celebration of faith which demonstrate the dramatic impulse in the Christian tradition. In pre-modern England many processions embraced strong elements of benediction and purification – especially in rural areas, where the protection of crops from evil influences was a priority. This was achieved through a ceremonial procession that eventually became known as 'beating of the bounds'. The tradition originated in a Christian form in 470 when Western Europe was alarmed by a series of prolonged natural disasters. At Vienne, France, Archbishop Mamertus ordered litanies to be said outdoors in solemn processions on Ascension Day or one of the three 'rogation' (Latin, *rogare*, 'to ask') days preceding it. By 747 this rite had arrived in England and eventually developed into an annual event with parishioners 'ganging' (Old English for 'going' or 'walking') around the edge of the parish. In different locations these may be known as Gang Days, Cross Days or Grass Days.

Beating of the Bounds – a procession through Leyton Marshes, London, May 2009. Photograph by Mark Lewis.

Beating the bounds rituals had two purposes. Firstly, they were undertaken by the clergy, choir and parishioners for the purpose of asking God's blessing upon the new crops, during which psalms (usually 100, 103 and 104) were sung and prayers chanted. Secondly, they had an administrative function of renewing a mental map of the parish. They also represented a public affirmation of the physical and social limits of the community (Bushaway 1982: 82). Confirming the exact physical limits of parish boundaries was essential in the event of disputes about property and land rights. To this end such biblical texts as 'Cursed be anyone who moves a neighbour's boundary marker' (Deuteronomy 27:17) were commonly used in the preaching.

The parish boundary was marked by stones which were literally 'beaten' with peeled willow wands to visibly confirm their position and establish them in the communal memory. The beatings were also considered to protect new crops from evil spirits and it has been suggested that the practice may have been regarded in rural folklore as a way of promoting productivity by awakening the sleeping earth (Christian 1966: 59). Breaks were taken during the walk at notable trees where gospel readings would be given. The names 'Gospel Oak' or 'Vicar's Oak' in various parts of Britain are a vestigial

Beating the bounds at Oxford. Photograph by Doc Rowe.

reminder of this practice. Other natural landmarks would be encountered, such as prominent stones, streams or ponds. These were physically impressed upon the children, usually by ducking, or even by ritually beating or whipping them. Boys could occasionally be upended and 'bumped'. But whatever strategy was used, it was usually followed by a treat. The punishment of an offending boy was often reserved by his father for the day of the perambulation when he would receive a substantial lashing (Addy 1895: 128), suggesting that there could also have been an element of social control built into the proceedings. However, there was generally a celebratory mood at the end of the event and participants were usually rewarded with 'ganging beer' and 'rammalation biscuits'.

Sometimes physical obstructions could be encountered, but no obstacle was considered too difficult to negotiate. At St Mary's, Leicester, the perambulation passed through some private houses which happened to be across the parish boundary and owners were required to leave their doors open to admit the beaters (Hunt 1954: 82–3). At Crompton, Lancashire someone was required to swim across a reservoir and then crawl through an outlet tunnel (Christian 1966: 60). Nowadays   beat the bounds of Her Majesty's Tower Liberty, every three years on Ascension Day, and the proceedings require a boat to be taken out to the middle of the River Thames. Here a choirboy is held over the side to beat the water, because part of the parish boundary falls in the centre of the river.

The Wilkes Walk, Leighton Buzzard, 2010. Photograph by Terry Warburton.

Some perambulations had a distinctly local flavour, such as Lichfield, Staffordshire, where on Ascension Day all local houses had greenery pushed through their letter boxes in the morning. The Dean and Chapter then processed around the Cathedral Close carrying elm boughs, stopping at eight places where prayers were said and psalms sung. On re-entering the Cathedral, the branches were dipped in the font, laid around it and a benediction given (Urlin 1915: 113–4). The custom appears to have lapsed in recent years. The enclosures of the eighteenth and nineteenth centuries put an end to many of these perambulations. However, towards the end of the twentieth century beating of the bounds was revived in different parts of the country.

Rogationtide also sees another curious memorial procession in the form of the annual Wilkes' Walk at Leighton Buzzard, Bedfordshire. On Rogation Monday the choir and clergy of All Saints' church, together with the clerk and trustees of the Wilkes' charity, process to the almshouses on North Street which were founded by Edward Wilkes in the seventeenth century. A hymn is sung followed by a prayer and an anthem. A member of the choir is then 'upended' while the will is read out by the clerk. Money is given to residents of the almshouse and refreshments are provided at the Market Cross near the church. The requirement of a child to make a head-stand is a curious feature of this custom and clearly derives from the practice of 'bumping' youngsters at boundary points in beating of the bounds (Roud 2006: 247).

Services of blessing

Crop blessings were traditionally the justification for the Rogationtide perambulations but many rural communities evolved their own distinctive ceremonies. Parishioners regularly processed around the fields or the congregation gathered in the churchyard and looked towards the open country while asking for God's blessing on the fields, those working in them, and the crop that would result. For Christians there is also an element of thanksgiving in this action for it acknowledges God's presence, the bounty of the created order and a dependence on God in all things. At Hever, Kent, the blessing of the fields was one of the most important Rogationtide customs and cherry orchards were also blessed at Newington, Kent on Rogation Sunday until very recently.

A most unusual but very practical method of blessing crops was sporadically undertaken at Welshpool, Powys. The Welshpool and Llanfair Light Railway provided transport for the vicar and his congregation on Rogation Sunday so that they could proceed across the countryside blessing the crops from the train. The last time this was undertaken was in May 2010 and the following year they performed the ritual from the canal (M Lister 2011, pers. comm. 30 August).

Wherever the local economy is dependent on a particular natural product or the livelihoods of local people are at stake, blessings and prayers of thanksgiving have been offered. Perhaps the most unusual example is the ceremony that took place until recently at St Botolph's Church, Lullingstone. The local castle was a silk farm, producing fine robes for customers including the royal family. Silkworm cocoons and silk products were annually taken to be blessed at the church, and similarly at St Michael's Abbey, in Farnborough, Hampshire. Honey has always been a highly valued product of nature and in its fermented form it becomes the prized ancient drink known as mead. St Bartholomew is the patron saint of beekeepers and honey-makers and the Blessing of the Mead still takes place at Gulval, Cornwall every year on his feast day (24 August). After a special service attended by the Worshipful Company of Mead Makers everyone processes to the Mead Hall where the vicar (who is also the Almoner of the Company), blesses the mead in a loving cup.

The raw material of beer is also acknowledged on Hop Hoodening Day at Canterbury, which is a harvest festival for the hop growers of East Kent. On

Hop Hoodening service at Canterbury Cathedral. Photograph by Canterbury Cathedral.

the First Saturday in September a procession makes its way through the precincts into the Cathedral led by the Hop Queen in a Hop Bower and closely followed by country dancers and Morris Men. Two Hooden Horses are also part of the sequence. They are all greeted at the door of the Cathedral by a member of the senior clergy and process down the main nave for the service. A 'bine' of hops is blessed by the Dean. During the service the Morris sides dance in front of the altar along with the Handbell Hoodeners and the local country dance team. This colourful celebratory custom has been established since 1954.

Blessing of the Waters

The maritime communities have always blessed and given thanks for the harvest of the sea. Public blessing rituals still occur at various fishing ports around the coast, although they are not always maintained on an annual basis. At Folkestone, Kent, for example, the vicar of St Peter's church leads the blessing of the sea and fisheries on the Sunday nearest to St Peter's Day (29 June). In late July the annual Blessing of the Waters, which dates from

1657, takes place during the Oyster Festival at Whitstable, Kent. This is held as near as possible to the Feast Day of St James (25 July) as he is the patron saint of oystermen. Fishing nets are blessed in Great Yarmouth, Norfolk, at St Nicholas' church in October. Until recently, salmon nets were blessed at Norham on the River Tweed, before midnight on 14 February, just before the netting season opened. The first catch was traditionally given to the vicar. About mid-October the ceremony of Blessing the Fish Harvest takes place at St Oswalds's church, Flamborough Head, Yorkshire. The village church is decorated with lobster pots, nets and lines; fish from the previous day's catch are also displayed.

During Rogationtide at Mudeford, Hampshire, the vicar of All Saints' church is rowed out to sea to the bless the waters, leaving small crosses floating there. Two ceremonies of sea blessing given by the Greek Orthodox Church are an interesting departure from the Anglican tradition. At Hastings, Suffolk, a large cross decked with flowers is dipped into the sea three times to ensure good catches during the forthcoming fishing season. Similarly during Epiphany at Margate, Kent, the Greek Orthodox Archbishop of Thyateria and Great Britain throws a crucifix decorated with flowers into the sea, which is then brought ashore by a swimmer.

River blessings were once common practice and an impressive annual ceremony is the Blessing of the River Thames on London Bridge. On the Feast Day of the Baptism of Christ, members of the clergy and laity from St Magnus' church, City of London and Southwark Cathedral process to the centre of the bridge for a short service. Prayers are said for the people who work on the river, the work of the lifeboat service and for those who lost their lives in the water during the past year. Following the Greek Orthodox tradition, a large wooden cross is thrown into the river as a symbol of Christ's birth and baptism. A similar service of Blessing of the River Dart takes place at Kingswear and Dartmouth, Devon on Ascension Day. A curious revival from the nineteenth century is 'Cowslip Sunday' at Lambley, Nottinghamshire, where the local stream is blessed by the rector during an annual festival held on the first Sunday in May; cowslips are traditionally celebrated through decorating the church, a village procession and a day of entertainments.

Blessing of the boats

Boat blessings are especially well-supported, undoubtedly because of the unpredictable dangers that mariners confront while at sea. Prayers are offered for sailors and fishermen to protect them from the perils of the deep. One of the oldest of these coastal ceremonies was the Blessing of the Fishing Boats at Chesil Bank, Abbotsbury in Dorset. On 12 May, garlands were taken in

Blessing of the River Thames. Photograph by James Hatts.

procession down to the boats where they were blessed and taken out to sea by the fishermen. They were left as an offering on the water and marked the beginning of the fishing season. The fishing boats have now gone from Abbotsbury but they are still remembered with garlands set on wooden frames which are made by the local children and processed through the village to be placed at the War Memorial.

The spectacular Blessing of the Fleet at Brixham, Devon, first recorded in 1926 has endured many revivals and the service which occurs on a Sunday evening in late May now forms part of the Heritage Festival of the town (Roud 2006: 274). Other blessings take place at North Shields and Cullercoats, Tyneside on a Monday in May and at Whitby, Yorkshire on Ascension Day (see photograph overleaf). At Southampton, a ceremony dating back to the thirteenth century was revived in 1950 during which prayers are offered from a boat by a priest for the port's great liners and cargo ships. The world of pleasure-boating also receives a benediction when the Norfolk Broads are blessed by the Bishop of Norwich from the ruins of St Benet's Hulme Abbey, Horning in Norfolk on the first Sunday in August.

Animal blessings

Services of animal blessing are intended to praise and affirm the valuable contribution that animals and pets make to human lives. These are recent developments and although services are common in the United States, they have taken time to become established in animal-loving Britain, where only a modest number of parishes have provided them on an annual or occasional basis. Money is often raised from the ceremonies to support animal rescue organisations. Horses however, have fared better as a focus of benediction,

Blessing of boats at Whitby, North Yorkshire. Photograph by Doc Rowe.

probably because of their past importance in the lives of humankind. Traditionally, carriage horses were blessed at the beginning of the driving season and a blessing service was revived by a carriage club at Picton Castle, Haverfordwest, Pembrokeshire in April 2011.

The most renowned equestrian benediction takes place on Horseman's Sunday, the third Sunday in September at St John's church, Hyde Park, London. The vicar traditionally leads a cavalcade of horses and riders to the church in order to celebrate horse riding in the heart of London. A short service takes place on the forecourt where the horses are blessed. This custom was first established in 1968 to emphasise the need to maintain stables along the north of Hyde Park.

Well dressings and blessings

Springs and wells have been venerated and blessed throughout history in all religious traditions to celebrate water as a necessity of life. With the arrival of Christianity in Britain, the worship of water was forbidden, but most of the ancient wells were stripped of their pagan associations and re-dedicated to the Blessed Virgin Mary or one of the saints. The dressing of wells is a unique English custom which has been observed on Ascension Day since the Middle Ages and is particularly well established in Derbyshire. Certain local wells came to be honoured with elaborate floral decorations. Since the nineteenth century, pictures have been created with flower petals, berries, leaves, bark

Horseman's Sunday, Hyde Park London. Photograph by Victoria Neville.

and any materials of purely natural origin pressed onto a wooden base covered with soft clay. The images are generally religious in subject matter, although contemporary developments have begun to embrace more secular themes.

Tissington in Derbyshire has had the longest tradition of well-dressing. Traditionally, the day begins with a thanksgiving service in the church, after which the parish priest, choir and congregation process to the five wells which are each blessed in turn. The connection of the custom with Ascension Day is tenuous but may relate to a prolonged drought in the seventeenth century during which the five wells at Tissington continued to supply water. The village community gathered together in thanksgiving on Ascension Day and thereafter the custom took on a Christian association, and became a part of the annual observance of the feast. Another story maintains that its well dressings began in 1350 when the villagers escaped the Black Death and credited their survival to the purity of their water (Hole 1978: 323–4).

With improved water supply to the district in the early nineteenth century, taps began to supplant the wells. Wirksworth was the first village in Derbyshire to have piped water in 1827, and this was celebrated annually

A well-dressing at Tissington, Derbyshire.in 2012. Photograph by Glynn Williams.

with well-dressings which still continue to be prepared at the end of May. Youlgrave quickly followed with its ceremony on the Saturday nearest to St John the Baptist's Day (24 June). Other well-dressings take place on variable dates at many other Derbyshire locations including Bakewell, Barlow (see photograph opposite), Brackenfield, Etwall, Millthorpe and Tideswell, and there are similar events in other parts of the country.

Fairs, football and dancing and church ales

Even in the consecrated domain of the dead, various seasonal entertainments, sports and revelries took place during the Middle Ages. Despite various protestations from senior clergy, churchyards were considered legitimate public spaces and the accepted site of fairs, feasts and sporting activities. However, the church precincts would have much more open in pre-modern times and the north side, generally considered the unholy domain where suicides and criminals were buried, was the favoured location for celebrations. Typically, on Sunday people went to Matins and Mass in the morning and spent the rest of the day indulging in sports and amusements in the church precincts. At large-scale gatherings these could include dancing contests, bowls, football, humorous races and competitions accompanied by all kinds of music. Bull-baiting and horse racing were also

Well-blessing ceremony at Barlow, Derbyshire in 2012 Photograph by Mike Abberley

common. In some Welsh parishes there was a particular preference for the cruel sport of cock-fighting – in Montgomeryshire cockpits survived in two churchyards as late as 1888 (Owen 1896: 155–6; Dymond 1999: 491). If a church was blessed with a saintly shrine or relic, large crowds of pilgrims could be guaranteed for the period of an anniversary so the demand for food, drink and amusements was considerable. Minstrels, Morris dancers, jugglers, peddlers and other traders helped to supply that demand, and a pilgrimage easily evolved into a fair.

Patronal festivals and parish wakes

The greatest celebrations were usually reserved for the anniversary of the dedication of a parish church. A patronal festival was held in honour of the patron saint and generally observed as a local secular holiday. This event was known as a wake, feast or revel. The word 'wake' means a vigil and derives from the ancient custom of 'waking' or 'watching' in the church overnight before a holy day, which would usually be spent in revelry. As early as 601, St Gregory recommended that the anniversary of the dedication of a church should be a festival celebrated 'with religious joyousness' (Tyack 1899: 68). These festivities would have included processions led by images of the saint, as well as general sports, feasting, fairs and other amusements.

In Wales the patronal festival was known as a 'mabsant' (literally, 'saint's son'). These were extraordinarily rowdy and lively affairs that were well established by the seventeenth century and surprisingly resistant to the purging efforts of the Reformers (Suggett 1996). Every kind of entertainment featured at these events and even the church building could be invaded for feasting or boisterous games. In Cardiganshire for example, wrestling matches occurred in some of the upland chapels! These wakes were characterised by disputes and settling of old scores. On the Welsh border fights were used to settle all quarrels of the past year, and some of the more spectacular evening battles lived long in the communal memory (Leather

1912: 156). Dancing was an almost mandatory pastime practised with great intensity at parish wakes and other feast days in Wales, and considered by Benjamin Malkin to be 'universal' in Radnorshire (Malkin 1804: 269–70). In north-west Wales another layer of revelry evolved in the form of 'Relic Sundays'. These were three special Sundays in the summer where parishioners focussed on the shrines and relics of their patron saints, seeking spiritual protection after making offerings and trying to divine their future (Suggett 1996: 96).

Wakes were enormously popular but sometimes events could get out of hand and the Reformation attempted to tone down both the Welsh and English celebrations. In the fourteenth century an act had been passed forbidding markets and fairs in churchyards and other injunctions followed, but they were not particularly effective in maintaining order. In the sixteenth century fines were dispensed to anyone caught playing games such as football or wrestling. Nevertheless it seems that even these measures had minimal impact as a deterrent and the playing of games in churchyards continued well into the nineteenth century. An Act of Convocation was passed in 1536, ordering that every parish should observe its patronal festival on the first Sunday in October irrespective of the official saint's day. However this was quickly doomed to failure and local churches were determined to keep their own saint's day as at present. By the beginning of the nineteenth century, the tradition of wakes had lost most of its religious connotations and become a regular summer holiday, particularly in the Midlands and northern counties.

Church Ales

An important part of community life in the Middle Ages was the parish feast known as a 'church ale'. By Tudor times they were a regular event on Sundays and were also held at Easter, May Day and patronal festivals, although Whitsuntide gradually became the favoured season for holding these feasts. The primary purpose of the 'Whitsun Ales' was to raise money for maintaining the church fabric or to provide alms for the poor, by providing a spirited social gathering for parishioners. The churchwardens were charged with the task of brewing the ale from malt, which was either bought from parish funds or received as gifts from the congregation. In many parishes a 'church-house' containing all the necessary equipment and utensils was made available for this purpose and their existence explains why well-established inns may be found close to many village churches.

Church ales were very popular in the north of England, where it was the practice to hold them in tents and booths in the churchyard. In other parts of the country they usually took place in a large empty barn. A Lord and Lady of the Ale might be elected to preside over the festivities, supported by a steward, sword-bearer and other officials. Entertainments were diverse, from music, song and dance to bowls, card-playing, and the baiting of bulls, bears and badgers, with food and ale available in generous quantities. The duration of these ales varied considerably but up to two days was not unusual.

Inevitably, events could become disorderly. The Reformers took great moral offence to the quantities of alcohol being consumed and the subsequent unruly behaviour. Even as early as the thirteenth century, hard-line bishops were forbidding clergy to attend ales or similar festivities (French 1884: 83–5). Various futile attempts to suppress church ales were made by the Puritan authorities in the seventeenth century, but most parish clergy seemed to be remarkably tolerant and recognised that when ales were in full swing, church services were better attended than on other days. Other forms of church ale were held as minor festivities, for specific purposes. 'Clerk ales' for example, were intended to boost the meagre salaries of the parish clerks. A 'help ale' or 'bid ale' was a festive gathering to raise funds for a parishioner or family who had fallen on hard times. A 'christening ale' gave an opportunity for happy families to celebrate a baptism and a 'bride ale' was funded for those too poor to provide their own wedding feast. A 'give ale' was held as the outcome of a bequest which was designed to keep alive the memory of the deceased donor (Hackwood 1909: 53–4).

Church ales began to wane by the nineteenth century, although a Whitsun Ale that continued for several days was held every seven years at Woodstock, Oxfordshire and lasted until about 1850. The demise of these gatherings was partly due to puritanical ideals holding sway, although changes in the system of parish rating, charging rents for church pews and other fund-raising activities also contributed to their decline (Hole 1978: 327–8). The ales were probably the precursors of the bazaars and sedate fêtes which are now regular annual features of church culture (Barnes 1959: 106). However, there has been at least one recent attempt at reviving a church ale following the traditional model, at Wivenhoe, Essex, in September.

Rushbearing customs

In spite of the secularisation of the wake, one of its most enduring religious survivals has been the custom of 'rushbearing'. This dates back to the medieval period when church floors were unpaved and the aisles were thickly strewn with rushes as a sweet-smelling protection against the penetrating damp of packed earth floors. The carpet of rushes was renewed on an annual basis. By the end of the eighteenth century the custom had developed into a religious ceremony and become an essential part of the patronal festival of the church. The rushes were brought to the church in a procession, carried in bundles by young women, usually dressed in white. Many villages used elaborately decorated rushcarts accompanied by Morris

dancers and children carrying garlands. The garlands were later hung in the church after the rushes had been laid on the floor. The custom had declined by the beginning of the nineteenth century, as most church floors were then paved with stone.

Rushbearings were formerly common all over England but a few have survived in a symbolic form as a community procession and celebration, mostly in the north. At Grasmere, Cumbria, the custom still survives despite the fact that the church was paved in 1820. Six girls dressed in green, known as the 'rush maidens', , carry a linen sheet which contains the rushes. Some rushes are fashioned into emblems called 'rushbearings', which are of varying shape, such as cross, harp and maypole. Traditionally, many of these constructions had direct biblical allusions, such as Moses in the bulrushes, the Star of Bethlehem and David's harp. Perhaps some of these designs may be a survival of the pre-Reformation Miracle Plays (Rawnsley 1953: 6–7). Typically, the procession is followed by a church service. The rushbearings are placed on shelves in the church and the children receive pieces of gingerbread stamped with the name of St Oswald who is the patron saint of the church. The ceremony is held on the Saturday nearest 5 August, St Oswald's Day.

At Ambleside, Cumbria on the Saturday nearest St Anne's Day (26 July) adults and children carry wooden frames covered with decorations of flowers and rushes including two rush pillars which are nearly ten feet high. Other

Opposite: *Rushbearing at Grasmere, Ambleside, Cumbria. The 'Rush maidens' entering the church.*

Right: *Rushcart at Sowerby Bridge, West Yorkshire.*

Photographs by Averil Shepherd.

rushbearings occur in Cumbria at St Columba's church, Warcop, (St Peter's Day, 29 June), St Mary and St Michael's Church, Urswick, usually held on the Sunday nearest to St Michael's Day (29 September), and at Sowerby Bridge, West Yorkshire (on the first weekend in September). A rare example of this custom in the south, takes place at St Mary's Redcliffe, Bristol on Pentecost Sunday when the church is extravagantly decorated with flowers and herbs. The occasion is known locally as 'Rush Sunday' and was first recorded in 1493. The rushbearing procession is attended by the Lord Mayor of Bristol and other civic dignitaries.

The rushbearing custom has survived more widely in the modified form of 'hay-strewing' on both the pews and the floor of the church to make it warm and dry. On the Sunday nearest St Peter's Day, grass is strewn at Wingrave, Buckinghamshire as a result of a legacy of 1798. A woman lost her way in nearby fields and would have died of cold except for the sound of the village church bells which finally guided her way back to safety. Upon her death, the woman left a field to the parish, stipulating that rushes should be cut from the land annually and strewn over the floor as a thank offering (Spicer 1954: 91). The rush and hay-strewing customs lack the public processional element of rushbearing but were extremely common until the mid-twentieth century in many village churches, especially in Leicestershire. It is maintained at Langham in Rutland on the Sunday following the Feast of St Peter (29 June). At one time the hay came from a meadow called Bell Acre. A rush-strewing service also takes place at the remote St Stephen's Church Forest Chapel in Macclesfield Forest, Cheshire, on the 1st Sunday after 12th August.

Pilgrimages

Local processions are a powerful visible demonstration of Christian witness. However, a more demanding way of signifying faithful commitment is through pilgrimage. A pilgrimage is a journey or search of great moral or spiritual significance which might be undertaken as an act of devotion, penitence or thanksgiving. In the Middle Ages these spiritual journeys would often be physically exhausting and sometimes hazardous but, then as now, they demonstrated a desire for the miraculous which has 'been fertilised by the… ancient human desire to clothe beliefs in form and substance' (Purcell 1981: xi).

The Holy Land was always the greatest focal point of medieval pilgrimage, although the desire for healing encouraged less taxing domestic journeys to English shrines such as the birthplace of a saint or place where miracles were performed (see Chapter 1). The tomb of Thomas à Becket at Canterbury Cathedral, who was murdered in 1170, was the most popular goal for early pilgrims in England. His death led to a rush to acquire pieces of cloth soaked in his blood which were widely believed to cure blindness, epilepsy and leprosy. King Edward the Confessor lies in Westminster Abbey and he is the only English saint whose body still rests in its medieval shrine. Parish pilgrim groups still visit regularly and an annual national pilgrimage takes place in October.

The shrine at Walsingham Abbey, Norfolk, became a popular destination for pilgrims for it housed a sealed glass jar that was said to contain the milk of the Virgin Mary. By association water from the Walsingham spring also acquired a reputation for curing pains in the head and stomach. Pilgrimages to Walsingham Abbey still take place and the highlight is the candlelit Procession of Our Lady which takes place every Wednesday and Saturday evening between Easter and the end of October. Some ancient pilgrimages have seen revivals in recent years. For example, since 2008 pilgrims have visited the ruins of Hailes Abbey in Gloucestershire. In pre-Reformation times, this was a magnet for pilgrims because it housed the 'Holy Blood of Hailes' which was believed to be a relic of the Crucifixion. Pilgrims now come here for spiritual contemplation and a week of creative activities (Wilkinson 2010: 32).

However, the contemporary desire for spiritual insight has seen the introduction of new pilgrimages to sacred places. An annual Anglican pilgrimage to Glastonbury, Somerset, in June was first held by a few local churches in 1924 and continued until recently and groups of pilgrims still come in January to see the Holy Thorn blossom in St John's Churchyard. Another pilgrimage which began in the late twentieth century and has enjoyed considerable support takes place on the first Saturday of July every year at Bradwell, Essex. Here Christians follow in the footsteps of St Cedd who arrived in 653 to establish a monastic community. Pilgrims assemble at the Bradwell village church of St Thomas for opening worship and then walk to St Peter's Chapel to enjoy fellowship through a picnic followed by an open-air service.

Whitsun walks

Club-walking began in the nineteenth century when benefit or 'sick clubs' and various trading associations made a show of solidarity in their community through street processions. These usually ended with a short church service followed by a dinner. These were reminiscent of the early trade or guild processions and were promoted as being essentially healthy activities. Whit walks, which began as Sunday School outings, became important 'processions of witness' (Entwhistle 2012) and are still upheld at various locations in and around Manchester on Whit Sunday or during Whit Week. New clothes were always worn while children had their white clothes adorned with fresh flowers. Church groups walked in procession, carrying colourful banners accompanied with bands and hymns.

Female 'Friendly Societies' around the country traditionally provided help in times of need and their annual parades were a common feature of many towns. All of these societies have now been disbanded as a result of the welfare state provision, with the notable exception of the Neston Female Society, founded in 1814. A 'Ladies' Day walk' still takes place through the streets of Neston, Cheshire, on the first Thursday of June. They parade to the parish church for a service, carrying short white staves on which are tied a garland or posy of flowers, followed by choir, clergy and civic dignitaries.

Rents and Candle Auctions

A tangible example of the Church extending itself into the community could be seen through the renting of a piece of land that often belonged to the parish in order to raise money for the church or charitable causes. The land would be let for a specified period of time through the curious custom of a 'candle auction'. These were very popular in the seventeenth and eighteenth centuries and a minority have survived to the present day. At Aldermaston in

Building the Penny Hedge, Whitby. Photograph by Doc Rowe.

Berkshire, a meadow known as Church Acre is still let every third year. The auction is conducted by the vicar who begins by sticking a pin into a lighted candle about an inch below the flame. The last person to make a bid before the pin falls out, holds the land for the following three years (Williams 1949). The oldest candle auction in the country takes place at the Church of the Blessed Virgin Mary, Chedzoy, Somerset, where a piece of land, also called Church Acre, was given to the church on the condition that it was auctioned every 21 years to raise funds for repairs to the church. The auction is believed to date from the fifteenth century. A similar custom takes place on the first Monday in January at The George, Hubberholme, North Yorkshire and is known as 'The Landletting of the Poor's Pasture'; the income is distributed to the poor of the parish.

Possibly the strangest ecclesiastical observance involving the payment of a rent exists in the annual custom of constructing the Penny Hedge at Whitby, North Yorkshire, on the eve of Ascension Day. The process begins with driving about twelve wooden stakes into the beach near Boyes Staithe in the harbour. Willows are then woven into them to form a 'Penny (pennance) Hedge' that must be strong enough to withstand three high tides. The hedge is a remnant of a fence called a 'horngarth', which was probably intended to contain the cattle of Whitby Abbey or to protect the landing place on the sands which was used by the Abbey. The tenants at Whitby were charged

Mystery Play performed at Chelmsford Cathedral, 2010. Photograph by Chelmsford Cathedral.

with the task of building the Horngarth annually as part of their rent to the Abbey. The original date of this custom is uncertain but possibly originated in Saxon times and may be the oldest surviving manorial custom in England (Jeffrey 1923: 38–45; Turton 1909: 57–67).

Mystery and miracle plays

One of the greatest affirmations of faith in many major English cities was the drama of the medieval mystery and miracle plays. They were certainly spectacular annual events in Chester, York, Wakefield, Lincoln, Norwich and Coventry. Mystery plays were a dramatic way of bringing biblical stories and the Christian message alive on the streets to educate a largely illiterate population. They were viewed as popular entertainment by many, but were also occasions of civic pride and local unity. The subject matter of mystery plays focused on the representation of bible stories from the Creation to the Day of Judgement, while miracle plays specifically dwelt on the miraculous intervention of the saints into the lives of ordinary people. They originally developed from more dramatic parts of seasonal church services such as the Nativity or the Crucifixion.

The dramas were originally performed in the church, but later moved into the churchyard and eventually to the public marketplace. In 1210 a papal edict forbade the clergy to act on a public stage and thereafter the Mystery plays were staged by local craft guilds or 'mysteries' (Latin *misterium* meaning 'occupation') with different guilds each taking responsibility for a particular play. The earliest plays were performed in Latin and introduced by a herald who would give a broad synopsis of the events. A combination of amateur and professional actors would be involved, sometimes performing in the open or on wooden pageant wagons, enabling each performance to take place in a different location (Pollard 1927; Young 1933).

The mystery plays were suppressed during the Reformation and remained unknown until they were revived in the twentieth century. The first major revivals occurred in York and Chester in 1951 for the Festival of Britain and since that time many other productions have taken place. The Chester Mystery Plays are now considered to be one of the largest community events in Britain, and are performed in Chester Cathedral, Cheshire, every five years, with the most recent production taking place in 2013. New adaptations of the Coventry Mystery Plays, which are probably best known as the source of the 'Coventry Carol' (see Chapter 6), are now performed at various venues in the city. In 2010, a cycle of plays took place in Chelmsford Cathedral. A feature of modern Sunday worship is the increasing contemporary expression of faith in liturgical drama using biblical narratives or creatively exploring and modernising the original story.

Chapter Six

Festivals and customs of the Church year

The rhythm of the changing seasons integrates with the cycle of the church year and has always provided recurring opportunities to celebrate the Christian faith in worship. Here we look at the ways in which this unfolding sacred calendar has stimulated many national and local customs and traditions by which the faithful have observed, commemorated and celebrated certain events or occasions. The Christian calendar is divided into Advent, Christmas, Epiphany, Lent, Easter and concludes at Pentecost. The remainder of the year following Pentecost is known as Ordinary Time, from the word 'ordinal' which simply means 'counted time'.

Advent

The season of Advent (Latin, *adventus* meaning 'coming') looks forward to Christ's birth and incarnation so is appropriately the beginning of the Anglican liturgical year and commences on Advent Sunday, the fourth Sunday before Christmas. The first clear reference to a celebration of Advent occurs in the sixth century.

Advent lasts until Christmas Eve and is a season of waiting and expectation as well as a time of spiritual preparation for Christmas. Advent connects with the Sunday before Advent, known as 'Stir-up' Sunday in reference to the opening lines of the 'collect' of that day in the Book of Common Prayer of 1539 which begins: 'Stir up we beseech thee O Lord the wills of thy faithful people... '. In spiritual terms, this prayer reinforces the significance of Advent and the preparations for the season. In pre-Reformation times the season had all the austerity of Lent with the faithful urged to consume a restrained diet of fish rather than meat. It is still considered a time of reflection and penitence.

Lighting the Advent Wreath, St Mary's Church, South Woodford, 2012. Photograph by Mark Lewis.

There are no flowers decorating the church and the mood is one of solemnity.

Purple is the liturgical colour of the season for vestments, reflecting penitence and royalty. Special liturgies for Advent include 'services of light' which are informed by words from St John's Gospel: 'I am the light of the world. Whoever follows me will not walk in darkness, but will have the light of life' (John 8:12). These services date back to the time of the early Christians and the service usually begins in darkness with hand-held candles being lit by the congregation. The recent custom of celebrating 'Toy Sunday' is upheld by many churches during Advent. The theme of the service is usually 'generosity' and the children of the congregation present unwanted toys during the service, which are subsequently given to children in need.

The Advent Wreath

This period of waiting is often marked by the Advent Wreath, a garland of evergreens with four candles. Although the main symbolism of the Advent wreath is simply marking the progression of time, many churches attach themes to each candle, most often 'hope', 'faith', 'joy' and 'love'. Where a fifth white candle is used, it represents Jesus Christ as the light of the world and is lit on Christmas Day. To further heighten the sense of anticipation of Christ's coming during Advent, the church has given significance to each candle in the wreath. A candle is ceremonially lit on Advent Sunday, and the remaining candles are lit in the same way during the remaining three Sundays. The first known use of Advent wreaths is by Lutherans in sixteenth century Germany, although they may originate from pre-Christian customs in northern Europe (Seaburg 1983: 236). They are generally made from a circle of evergreen plants such as holly and ivy symbolising an eternal and unchanging God. The holly is also a symbol of the crown of thorns that Jesus Christ wore when he was crucified.

Various traditions have accrued in Advent season. Candle-lit processions take place at York Minster and St Paul's Cathedral, London. In many country parishes, notably in Warwickshire and Lincolnshire, it was customary to celebrate the joyful hopes of Advent by ringing peals throughout the season, sometimes beginning as early as 5.00 a.m. (Walters 1912: 139–40). St Nicholas' Day on 6 December falls in Advent and is the day when Boy Bishops are enthroned in some churches and cathedrals – see Chapter 2.

Christmas

Carols and carol services

The English Christmas did not become established until the year 1000, and gradually built on earlier pagan midwinter festivals. For centuries, carol singing has become the first public indication that Christmas is approaching. The word carol or *carole* is a medieval word of French and Anglo-Norman origin, believed to mean a dance song or a circle dance accompanied by singing. Although carols are traditionally associated with Christmas they represent a genre of song that is also sung at other times during the liturgical year. Christmas carols in English first appear in a 1426 work of John Awdlay, a blind chaplain from Haghmon, Shropshire and were probably sung by groups of 'wassailers', who went from house to house (Miles 1912: 47–8). The customary time to begin singing carols was St Thomas's Day, 22 December (Wright and Lones 1940 Vol 3: 225).

Christmas carols remained popular but were banned by the Puritans in 1647. Although Christmas was revived under Charles II carols with their distinctive verse and refrain did not became fashionable again until after 1822. Singing carols in church was instituted in a wooden shed that served as Truro Cathedral, Cornwall on Christmas Eve 1880 by Bishop Edward W. Benson, who was later Archbishop of Canterbury. The service occurred in the form that is now known as the Ceremony of Nine Lessons and Carols. The Bishop is said to have modelled the event on medieval vigil services – but with the primary purpose of keeping men out of pubs on Christmas Eve. Another famous Christmas custom is the singing of the Coventry Carol at Coventry Cathedral, which has been sung since the time of Henry VI when it was part of a play where Bethlehem's women sang before Herod's soldiers entered to slay the children.

The Nativity Play

The nativity play has always been the most enduring way of presenting the Christmas story and remains popular in all churches and schools. St Francis of Assisi and his followers performed a play during Midnight Mass in Greccio on Christmas Eve 1223, to educate the illiterate local population of the significance of Jesus Christ, emphasising that like them he was born into a poor family. The setting was life-size with live animals and this is sometimes credited as the first Nativity play. The tradition of a displaying a Nativity scene in church or home started in Germany in the 1600s. However, more formal Nativity plays have featured in Christian worship since medieval mystery plays. The twelfth to nineteenth pageants of the full forty-eight cycle York Mystery Plays enact the Nativity story – see Chapter 5.

The Christingle service

Christingle services are a recent feature of the Anglican Church and are celebrated during the Christmas season. The Christingle (from the German

Christingles prepared for the service at St Mary's Church, South Woodford, London, 2011. Photograph by Mark Lewis.

A Christingle Service at St Mary's Church, South Woodford, London, 2011. Photograph by Mark Lewis.

Krist Kindl, meaning 'Little Christ Child' via its American corruption Krisskringle) is a symbolic object and has its origins in the Moravian Church. During Christmas 1747 Johannes de Watteville, the bishop at Marienborn, Germany, considered how he could educate children on the true meaning of Christmas in a fresh and lively way. He gave each child a lighted candle wrapped in a red ribbon, with a prayer that said 'Lord Jesus, kindle a flame in these dear children's hearts'. This was the first Christingle service. In 1968, John Pensom of The Children's Society introduced this service to the Anglican Church, where the custom spread rapidly. The Christingle consists of an orange, representing the world, with a lighted candle to represent Christ, the Light of the World. Sweets on cocktail sticks are placed around the candle representing God's bounty in providing the fruits of the earth.

Christmas Eve

Christmas Eve is the true start of Christmas and begins with the decoration of the churches. Since the early medieval period, it has been the custom to adopt the pagan practice of embellishing houses and churches with winter fruit-bearing plants such as holly, ivy and box evergreens. Mistletoe was considered to have strong healing qualities but was generally prohibited from churches, probably because of its Druidical connections (Tyack 1899: 131). However, there are records of it being presented at the altar of York Minster (Andrews 1890: 53) and there was an ancient custom bound up with magical beliefs at St Peter's, Wolverhampton. Mistletoe was placed on the altar where it was blessed by the priests and distributed to the people who believed it to be beneficial in curing fever (Wright and Lones Vol 3: 224). There is an ancient link between the Tree of Life and Jesus Christ and some churches use Christmas trees as decoration at Christmas time. Holly wreaths are still sometimes placed on graves at Christmas (Hunt 1954: 35).

On the afternoon of Christmas Eve a special service takes place at Cambridge University's King's College Chapel. This is the 'Ceremony of Nine Lessons and Carols', based on the pioneering example Bishop Edward W. Benson at Truro Cathedral in 1880, and features nine Bible readings accompanied by nine Christmas carols and other appropriate musical works. Listening to the King's College Chapel service became a popular domestic ritual after it was first broadcast in 1928 and today many churches throughout England, the United States and around the world hold their own versions of this. Carolling on Christmas Eve around local streets has always been especially popular, although it was a tradition in Devon during in the late nineteenth century for the choirs of various churches to go round parishes on this day, stopping at important homes to sing an anthem or carol where they could be rewarded with hot drinks (Cossins 1877: 68). Singing carols on the top of church towers was also an occasional practice, with notable instances at Newbury, Berkshire and Crondall, Hampshire (Vaux 1894: 223).

Midnight Mass and the Plygain Tradition

The first Christmas masses were first celebrated in Rome early on Christmas morning. In the fifth century another mass was celebrated in the middle of the night and between 400–1200 it was prescribed that this service was to be held when the rooster crowed at about 3.00 a.m.. Eventually, the mass shifted to midnight, possibly because of the popular belief that Jesus Christ was born at this time. The Midnight Mass that is popular in many Anglican churches is a nineteenth century revival and one of the busiest services of the year. The Christmas crib may be blessed at the service.

The most distinctive Welsh survival is the *Plygain* (from the Latin *pulli cantus* meaning 'cockcrow song') service formerly held at dawn in many parts of Wales and sometimes with Holy Communion. Upon arrival, at the church, lengthy carols were sung, usually unaccompanied. Different groups would take turns to perform and as soon as one finished another was ready to take their place. In some districts, processions would form before the service. At

Plygain Singing, in St Teilo's church, St Fagan's: National History Museum, Cardiff . Photograph by National Museum of Wales .

Tenby, Pembrokeshire for example, young men in the town used to escort the rector with lighted torches from the rectory to the church and after the service the procession was returned to the rectory (Miles 1912: 99). At St Asaph, Denbighshire, and elsewhere, *plygain* involved singing carols in procession around the church (Vaux 1894: 222). Coloured candles were often carried in the services and the church interiors would also be richly illuminated with candles.

Plygain was abandoned in most churches in Wales during the 1850s and although taken up by the non-conformist churches the services began to die out in the twentieth century (Trevelyan 1909: 28). Today the Plygain takes place in only a few localities and may occur anytime between mid-December and early January.

The joyful ringing of bells was another highlight of Christmas and the peal rung on Christmas Eve or Christmas Morning was sometimes known as the 'Virgin Chimes' (Tyack 1899: 104). A merry peal, known as 'ringing in Christmas' was a popular tradition in many parts of the country, usually at 5.00 a.m. (Denham 1895: Vol 2: 92; Cocks 1897: 280). A unique tradition that is still upheld at Dewsbury, Yorkshire, is the custom of ringing the 'Devil's Knell' on Christmas Eve to scare away the Devil who, reputedly, died when Christ was born (Henderson 1879: 66).

Christmas Day

Christmas morning is now usually celebrated with a Holy Communion service. However in pre-Reformation times the day was initiated with a stately ceremony at the end of Christmas Matins. This was the chanting of St Matthew's genealogy of Christ. The deacon, with three or more acolytes carrying tapers, a thurible and a processional cross, all in appropriate vestments, went in a procession to the rood loft, to sing this portion of the gospel (Rock 1853 Vol III pt 2: 214). However, all celebrations were rapidly curtailed when the Puritans banned Christmas celebrations in 1664. Christmas Day then became a day of fasting until celebrations were again permitted with the restoration of the monarchy in 1660.

Choristers had a welcome break from their routine on Christmas morning in some parishes, not least by singing carols from the top of the church towers. At Exeter Cathedral in the early nineteenth century, the choristers sang Psalm 100 in a candle-lit minstrel gallery (Cossins 1887: 34). At Ripon Cathedral, Yorkshire an old tradition of the choristers handing out red apples to members of the congregation on Christmas Day was revived in 1989. Each apple is stuck with a sprig of rosemary. The apple symbolises life and the rosemary is considered to be a reminder of the Virgin Mary who made the birth of Christ possible (P. Greenwell, pers. comm. 3 May 2012). The choristers each receive a small gratuity for their trouble.

Holy Innocents' Day

After Christmas Day the most important festival was the Day of the Holy Innocents, or 'Childermas', celebrated on 28 December. This feast day commemorated the slaughter of children by Herod (Matt. 2:16) although its impact has been lost in recent years. In Northern England it was considered an appropriate day to indulge children and hold parties for them and a curious custom at Exton, Rutland, permitted children to play in the church (Dryden 1911: 198). This was also the last day of the term of office of Boy Bishops – see Chapter 2. Mournful church services were held and in many parts of the country, there were muffled or half-muffled peals of bells (Wright and Lones 1940 Vol 3: 280–1). The liturgical colour was formerly black or violet and not surprisingly, this is a day that has numerous bad luck superstitions associated with it.

New Year's Eve

Watch Night services were held in churches and chapels on New Year's Eve. The services originated with the Moravian Church and the first was held in or about 1742 (Wright and Lones 1940 Vol 3: 288); thereafter they were encouraged by John Wesley, the founder of the Methodist Church as an opportunity for Christians to review the year that has passed, make confession and then prepare for the year ahead by making new commitments. A midnight peal was also rung on New Year's Eve in many parishes.

Epiphany

Epiphany (Greek *epiphaneia*, meaning 'manifestation') is celebrated on 6 January. Epiphany was first observed in the Eastern Church to mark the birth of Christ, but around 354, when Christmas became fixed at 25 December in Rome, the Eastern Church celebrated the feast as Christ's baptism. For the Western Church the festival commemorated the visit of the Three Wise Men to the infant Christ, and the revelation of the Son of God to the Gentiles. Outside the Church calendar it is known more widely as Twelfth Night, in relation to Christmas and the day when all decorations should be removed for fear of bad luck.

In the medieval period it was the custom in some churches and cathedrals, notably St Mary's Church, Cambridge, and St Nicholas Church, Norwich, for the dramatic ceremony of 'The Feast of the Star' to take place. This was performed to illustrate the visit of the Magi and their guidance by the Star of Bethlehem to the cradle of Christ. A star was suspended above the nave and made to move towards the sanctuary, guiding priests dressed as the Magi; as they approached the high altar a curtain opened to reveal a living child in a cradle, while 'three kings' were also in attendance (Bolingbroke 1892: 334–5).

In modern churches figures representing the Three Wise Men, or the Magi, are placed in some crib scenes especially those in churches or nearby church schools. Special Epiphany carols are sung at the services, and processions commemorating the Journey of the Magi take place in some of the cathedrals, notably at Salisbury, Manchester and Chichester.

The most impressive contemporary Epiphany event is the service of Holy Communion celebrated in the Chapel Royal, St James's Palace, when the traditional gifts of gold, frankincense and myrrh are offered on behalf of the Queen. The service is believed to date back to 600. It became a crown-wearing day in the fifteenth century, and the sovereign always attended the ceremony in person. Nowadays, the offerings are made by two gentlemen ushers to the Queen (Hole 1978: 255).

Plough Sunday and Monday

Before the time when winter wheat was sown in the autumn, ploughing used to begin again immediately after the Christmas period. In medieval times it

was still a time for festivities, ploughs were blessed, and in the corn-growing areas of eastern England, Plough Plays were performed. The money raised was put towards a plough light, a lamp in the church that was never allowed to go out. Plough Sunday is a traditional English celebration of the beginning of the agricultural year that has seen some revivals over recent years. Before farmers had their own ploughs, the communal plough was decked with ribbons and brought in to the village church. Then God's blessing would be asked for the work that it was to do and there would be prayers for the blessing of the land.

Ploughs were sometimes blessed in church on Twelfth Day, but the tradition was more common on the first Sunday after 6 January. After the service, the plough would be paraded around the village, usually with dancing and regular stops at local inns for refreshment. The farmers who were going to use it would give contributions towards the cost of its upkeep and to maintain the plough light and the church where it had been blessed. The custom still takes place around the country, notably at Exeter and Chichester Cathedrals and at Curry Mallet, Somerset where local tradesmen and farm workers bring their tools to the church and farmers take seed corn to be blessed, followed by the plough. In some communities, such as Goathland, North Yorkshire, the children of farming families carry the plough in procession. Plough Monday is the first Monday after 6 January, and was a further opportunity for blessings, plough plays and festivity among agricultural workers, particularly in the eastern counties. At Northwold in

Opposite and above: *Children carrying the plough at Goathland, North Yorkshire on Plough Monday. Photographs by Doc Rowe.*

Norfolk for example, the celebrations were revived during the 1980s and there is a procession from the Crown Inn to St Andrew's Church to bless the plough, which is followed by molly dancing and mummers plays.

Candlemas

As the year moves into Epiphanytide, the next major festival is Candlemas which is also known as the Presentation of Christ in the Temple or the Feast of the Purification of the Virgin Mary. It is celebrated on 2 February and commemorates Mary's visit to the Temple to present the infant Jesus forty days after his birth, as Jewish law demanded, and symbolising the prophecy of 'A light to lighten the gentiles' (Luke 2: 22–38).

Its name may derive from the custom, dating at least from the fifth century, of celebrating the day with candle-lit processions. At Candlemas services, candles are usually blessed, often in great quantity. Ripon Cathedral revived a spectacular medieval ceremony in 1964 which witnesses the burning of four thousand candles on the Sunday before Candlemas Day. In the medieval period, blessed candles were widely believed to be protective against fire, evil spirits and thunderstorms – and the more brightly they burned, the more

*The Cradle Rocking Ceremony at St Mary's Church, Blidworth,
Nottinghamshire, Photograph by Geoff Howard.*

powerful the protection (Wright and Lones 1938 Vol II: 119). It was
traditional for these to be lit and distributed to members of the congregation.

In spite of the Puritans' vigorous condemnation of this custom as 'popish' it
never really died away and it is still the practice to hand out candles during
the service in many churches. It was also customary on the eve of Candlemas
to take down any remaining Christmas decorations from house and church
and replace them with branches of box. Anxiety about the complete removal
of Christmas evergreens was so intense that many wealthy families sent their
servants to sweep out their pews on Candlemas Eve. Even a single leaf left in
a pew signified that someone might die in the coming year (Tyack 1899:
131). Other flowers, such as snowdrops, were particularly favoured for the
adornment of churches at Candlemas and became known as the Purification
Flower because it traditionally blossomed at this time (Hunt 1954: 30).

A unique ceremony that still takes place at Candlemas is the cradle rocking
ceremony at Blidworth, Nottinghamshire which commemorates the
Presentation of Christ in the Temple (Wright 1928: 46). The baby boy who
has been most recently baptised in the parish is chosen to represent the infant
Christ and is presented by his parents to the vicar; the baby is blessed and
ceremonially rocked for a few moments in a wooden rocking cradle covered
in flowers. This is believed to be a medieval custom which lapsed at the

The Women's Pancake Race at Olney, Buckinghamshire. Photograph by Doc Rowe.

Reformation but was revived in 1923 and continues to take place every year (Hole 1978: 80).

Shrove Tuesday

Shrove, meaning the 'shriving' or stripping of one's sins, was originally a day of spiritual preparation, through making confession and receiving absolution, before the beginning of Lent on the following day, Ash Wednesday. The religious observance of Shrove Tuesday is now rarely observed, although its original pre-Lent role is still apparent with the consumption of pancakes on this day. However, at the Church of St Peter and St Paul, Olney in Buckinghamshire, a traditional Shriving service still takes place after the world's oldest pancake race which features only women who have lived in the town for more than six months! In more austere times this was a riotous day for playing games and general gluttony, anticipating the forthcoming deprivations of the Lenten season. The custom of 'Clypping the Church' took place on this day (see chapter 2) and the 'pancake bell' was rung in many districts (see chapter 3).

Ash Wednesday

Ash Wednesday is the first day of Lent and occurs forty-six days before Easter. It is known as a moveable feast as its date varies depending on the date of Easter. Its name derives from the traditional ceremonies of the early Church, in which the faithful had ashes placed on their foreheads reminding them that they were from ashes and to ashes they would return. Penitents were usually dressed in sackcloth to symbolise their separation from the community during the Lenten period. This alludes to Christ's words: 'They would have repented long ago in sackcloth and ashes' (Matthew 11: 21). The ceremony still continues in many churches. Ash is also a sign of mourning and repentance to God. It was customary to obtain ash by burning the palms blessed on the Palm Sunday of the previous year.

Lent

Lent (short for *Lenten*, from OE *lencten*, meaning 'spring' or 'lengthen') is the period of forty days before Easter which commemorates the forty days Christ spent in the desert fasting and inwardly preparing for his public ministry. For Christians, it has always been a period of abstinence, penitence and spiritual preparation. In medieval times Lent was a period of great austerity, in which strict dietary regulations were observed, when no meat, eggs or dairy produce were to be consumed. Sexual relations were also forbidden, and marriages were generally proscribed during this period. Lenten discipline has been much more relaxed in recent times and the giving up of vices and favourite treats tend to be the most common forms of self-denial.

In the church building, everything is liturgically understated during Lent and usually there are no flowers on display. Plain wooden crosses where they are available are now generally used in place of silver. In some churches it is customary to follow the Catholic practice of covering crosses during Lent with opaque purple veils, because these have traditionally been regarded as signs of victory.

Mothering Sunday

Mothering Sunday, also called 'Mid-Lent' is the fourth Sunday in Lent, when motherhood is celebrated. It is also known as 'Refreshment Sunday' in honour of the Feeding of the Five Thousand, (Matt 14: 13–21) which was traditionally the Gospel reading for the day.

The name Mothering Sunday arose from the practice of young people, after they had left home for service, returning to their families with gifts although the day is not recorded for this purpose until the mid-seventeenth century. Another compelling theory points to the practice in medieval times of the faithful going in procession on this day to their cathedral or 'mother church' where they were baptised and present offerings. It has also been suggested that the frequent proximity of Mothering Sunday to Lady Day (25 March),

Palm Sunday procession with a donkey, St Margaret's Church, Rainham, Kent, 2012. Photograph by Tony Fairclough

which is the principal celebration of Mary, Mother of God, may also have a connection with the naming of the day (Kightly 1986: 172). However, it has always been a day when young people, who lived away from home, particularly servants and apprentices, could be briefly reunited with their families and offer simple gifts to their mothers. The day is still celebrated enthusiastically in this way, with family communion services and often with a distribution of daffodils or other seasonal flowers given by children to their mothers at the end of the service.

Holy week

Palm Sunday

Holy week begins with a celebration of Christ's triumphal entry into Jerusalem, seated on a donkey while the people waved palm branches and shouted 'Hosanna' (meaning 'save us please!'). The distinctive ceremonies of the day are the blessing of palms and many churches have a procession in or around the church, sometimes with a donkey taking the lead, while the congregation sing songs of praise and wave palm leaves. There is usually a reading of the 'Liturgy of the Passion' (Matt. 26:14 to 27:66). The blessed palms are distributed to the people in the form of crosses, where they are taken home and carefully kept until Ash Wednesday the following year, when they should be reverently burned. They were also kept safely in the belief that they had protective powers, a practice contemptuously dismissed by the Puritans. Reformers under Henry VIII allowed the rites to continue as long as the celebration remained a commemoration and was not intended to invest the palm crosses with any sanctity (Hutton 1996: 183).

Palm Sunday in England was traditionally called Olive or Branch Sunday, and also known as Sallow, Willow or Yew Sunday. These names represent the local replacements for the traditional palm branches. Willow and hazel were especially favoured because their buds and catkins were regarded as a symbol of the ripening spring (Hutton 1996: 184). In many parts of the country, Palm Sunday was also known as Blossom or Flowering Sunday, from the custom of decorating the graves of friends and relatives with flowers. Various church doles have also taken place on Palm Sunday in certain Herefordshire parishes – see Chapter 4.

Maundy Thursday

This day commemorates the Last Supper of Jesus Christ with the Apostles. It is derived from the old French *mandé,* from the Latin *mandatum*, meaning a command. Jesus said 'A new commandment I give unto you, that you love one another; as I have loved you', (John 13: 34) to explain to the Apostles the significance of his action of washing their feet. The most important service of the day incorporates the act of foot-washing and the ancient custom of 'Stripping the Altar'.

The officiating priest ceremonially washes the feet of others and typically, twelve persons chosen as a cross-section of the community. The service concludes with a procession taking the Blessed Sacrament to a tabernacle or an altar of repose, usually in a side chapel. The altar, representing Christ is later stripped bare as a reminder of how he was stripped of his garments and is symbolic of the humiliation he endured at the hands of the soldiers. All candles are ritually extinguished, ornaments, linen and books are removed and the church is plunged into darkness. It was formerly the custom in some churches on this day to wash the altars with wine and water and scrub them with birch besoms (Hutton 1996: 187). This would have been undertaken as an act of purification and a reminder to the faithful that they should approach and receive Holy Communion with pure hearts.

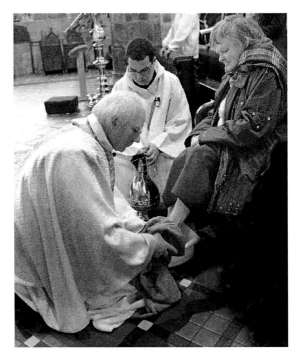

Bishop John washes the feet of Eleanor, at St. Giles, Wrexham, on Maundy Thursday, 2007. Photograph by Brian Roberts.

The most famous custom is the Royal Maundy offering of 'alms' to deserving senior citizens. This ancient ceremony dates back to the thirteenth century when the royal family took first part in Maundy ceremonies, to distribute money and gifts and to recall Christ's simple act of humility by washing the feet of the poor. Henry IV began the practice of relating the number of recipients of gifts to the sovereign's age, and it became the custom of the sovereign to perform the ceremony. The service at which this takes place rotates around cathedrals in England and Wales and although foot-washing was discontinued in the nineteenth century, a white purse containing special Maundy coins are now distributed, which are legal tender. A somewhat diminished version of this alms-giving custom was observed at Exeter Cathedral in the nineteenth century when the vergers took large baskets or 'maunds' of copper coins and distributed them to hundreds of children waiting outside (Vaux 1894: 237).

Good Friday

The Friday before Easter is the anniversary of the Crucifixion. It has always been a day of fasting, abstinence, and penance. The altar remains bare. No bells are rung and in medieval times, rattles were used to summon the faithful instead (Duffy 1992: 28-9). Services have always been solemn and reflective, consisting primarily of the veneration of the Cross, with the chanting of the 'Reproaches' or the Litany. Following medieval custom, Holy Communion is not usually celebrated on Good Friday although sometimes elements previously consecrated are distributed. In some churches, perambulations take place around the church with different readings at the fourteen 'Stations of the Cross'. The 'Three Hours' service is often held from noon until 3:00 p.m., and consists of seven sermons or meditations on the seven last words of Christ. Children's services are also held in some churches, during which hot cross buns are distributed. Some parishes join together for a 'Walk of Witness' on Good Friday morning when a large cross is processed through the local streets. A few parishes have revived the tradition of making this processional cross from the stripped branches of a Christmas tree, retained from previous festivities. Many parish doles are also distributed in the morning – see Chapter 4.

Before the Reformation it was customary in many county churches to erect an Easter sepulchre constructed from wood, in commemoration of Christ's entombment and resurrection. This was placed near the altar and contained an image of Christ, usually holding a cross. The sepulchre was placed within a recess in the north wall of the chancel, although several churches built permanent stone structures, notably in Lincolnshire, Nottingham and Norfolk (Sheingorn 1987). Candles were lit around the sepulchre, burial clothes adorned it, and parishioners would keep a vigil until early Easter morning at the first Mass. A contemporary custom, which possibly developed from the Easter sepulchre is the display of an Easter Garden in which Christ's tomb is prominent; a stone is placed across the entrance before Easter, and rolled away on Easter morning.

During the medieval period a crucifix was unveiled and placed in front of the altar followed by a ceremony which was popularly known as 'Creeping to the Cross'. The clergy, followed by the parishioners would make their way on knees to a cross and kiss it. This was followed by communion using one of the hosts consecrated on the Thursday (Feasey 1897: 114–20). Afterwards the priest and his assistants, all bare-footed, would ceremonially wrap the crucifix in fine fabrics and place a representation of the dead Christ in a 'sepulchre', together with a box containing the consecrated wafers from the previous day. The rite was banned as part of the Reformation under Elizabeth I although even as late as the end of the eighteenth century at Tenby in Pembrokeshire, the elderly were in the habit of walking barefoot to church on that day, suggesting an isolated remnant of this custom (Vaux 1894: 237).

Holy Saturday or Easter Even

This day celebrates the mystery, the death and resurrection of Jesus Christ. Evening church services are held in total darkness before the candles are lit to proclaim Jesus Christ's rising. In the medieval period, every light in the church would have been ritually extinguished; worshippers would witness a

A Good Friday Walk of Witness, Farnham, Surrey. Photograph by Mary Clarke of Churches Together in Farnham.

'New Fire' of coals or woods, traditionally lit with flints or directly from the sun with a 'burning glass'. This was then blessed and censed then a large taper was kindled from it and carried to illuminate a procession to the font, where the water for baptisms would be also be blessed (Hutton 1994: 24; Cox 1913: 54–5). Easter Even was traditionally the favoured day for group baptisms, while 'font-hallowing' ceremonies were also regularly performed (Dyer 1900: 159). In contemporary churches, baptisms and confirmations sometimes take place and customarily the members of the congregation renew their baptismal vows on Holy Saturday.

This ceremony still remains popular in both Anglican and Roman Catholic churches and many parishes still follow the tradition of burning a fire outside the church porch. The 'Paschal' candle is lit from the fire and decorated with various signs of the life of Christ. However, in some Anglican churches the lighting takes place at dawn on Easter Day. There follows the 'Progression of Light' as the candle is processed down through the nave and then an ancient hymn of praise, the *Exultet* is sung. The Paschal candle signifies the light of Jesus Christ that he brings into darkness and is prominently displayed on a post in the chancel where it remains until Ascension Day. The readings were traditionally heard by candle light, before the *Gloria* was sung and the

Lighting the Paschal candle from the New Fire, Holy Saturday at St John the Baptist Parish Church, Midsomer Norton and Clandown in Somerset.

church lights were illuminated once again. Fresh fires of charcoal or other fuel were sometimes prepared, lighted and even consecrated on this day.

Easter

Easter or the 'Feast of the Resurrection' is the greatest and oldest feast of the Church and celebrates the Resurrection of Christ after the crucifixion. The dating of Easter was always a source of great controversy and division in the early Church and is determined by the Paschal Full Moon, its extreme limits being 21 March and 25 April. The festival coincides with the Jewish Passover and in Europe it fused with elements of pagan spring festivals, celebrating new life. The Resurrection mood was always confirmed in many churches through rich displays of flowers and evergreens such as yew and box on Easter Day (Wright and Lones Vol 1 1936: 100) and the Use of Sarum prescribed the blessing of herbs sprinkled on the altar which would have added fragrance to the joyful atmosphere (Hutton 1996: 195).

In pre-Reformation England the first ceremony of the day was the opening of the sepulchre before dawn. This was the practice at Durham Cathedral while the anthem 'Christ is Risen' was sung (Hutton 1996: 195). The Host was brought out as Jesus was taken from the tomb, and placed in a tabernacle in the centre of the church (Duffy 1992: 30). A short dramatic dialogue was given, based on the conversation between the Angel and the two Marys outside the empty tomb (Smolden 1946: 1–17). Holy Communion would follow, sometimes at an early hour and, up to the sixteenth century, the Lenten fast was only finished when the Easter Mass had concluded (Duffy 1992: 93). In some contemporary churches, open-air sunrise services are held but the mid-morning Eucharist is the high point of Holy Week and this is when Easter eggs are distributed to children. Several charitable food customs are associated with Easter Day. Distributions of cakes were made in some parishes often by the parish clerks after the service (Vaux 1894: 241–2) and in some Shropshire villages the poor of the parish traditionally feasted in the church (Addy 1913: 332–3).

Ascensiontide and Rogation Week

Rogation Days

The word 'Rogation' (from the Latin, *rogare*, meaning 'to ask') was applied to this period of the liturgical year because the Gospel reading for the previous Sunday included the passage 'Ask and you shall receive' (John 16: 24). The Sunday itself was often called Rogation Sunday as a result, and marked the start of a three-week period ending on Trinity Sunday. The Rogation Days or Cross Days are the Monday, Tuesday and Wednesday before Ascension Day. These were prescribed as days of prayer and fasting and religious processions and perambulations such as 'Beating of the Bounds' took place through the fields to ask for blessings on crops and to confirm parish boundaries - see Chapter 5.

Ascension Day

Ascension Day or Holy Thursday, celebrates the Ascension of Christ to heaven after forty days on earth following the Resurrection. In some Catholic traditions this was graphically symbolised by a ritual in which a statue of Christ was lifted through a hole in the church roof followed by a flaming straw figure of Satan which was cast down through it. The Paschal candle was lit for the last time and removed to symbolise the ascent of Christ to heaven and church bells would ring out again. London churches were uniquely decked with garlands for Ascension Day. Some towns had processions and at Durham Cathedral the clergy processed around the city carrying gold and silver crosses and the relics of saints (Hutton 1996: 279). Beating of the Bounds usually takes place on Ascension day (see Chapter 5) although contemporary devotional customs for this day are rare. However, since 1902 the Choir of St John's College, Cambridge have ascended the Chapel Tower at noon on Ascension Day to sing Praetorius's Ascension Day

Carol. Communion services are now held in parish churches to celebrate Ascension Day.

May Day

Few Church ceremonies lay claim to the first day of May, undoubtedly because of its strong pagan associations. However, at 6.00 a.m. robed choristers from Magdalene Church School in Oxford walk to the top of Magdalen Tower singing a hymn, the *Hymnus Eucharisticus*. This is a tradition that spans over five hundred years, and ostensibly, commemorates Henry VII (Judge 1986: 15–40). The singing is followed by general revelry including Morris dancing and impromptu music.

A similar event takes place on Durham Cathedral tower where an anthem is sung from each of the three sides of the tower to commemorate the Battle of Nevilles' Cross between David II of Scotland and Edward III of England on 17 October 1346. This is believed to recall the attempts to build up the morale of English soldiers by bell-ringing and masses sung from the parapets. The west side of the tower is not used as a mark of respect to a chorister who once fell to his death from there (Ditchfield 1896: 121–2). At Charlton-on-Otmoor, Oxfordshire, a curious May Day custom involved the construction of a huge garland which is carried to the church by children singing May carols. There it was sprinkled with holy water and placed on the fifteenth century rood screen. The tradition was first recorded in 1816 and is probably an early May garland custom that became caught up in an ecclesiastical context (Roud 2006: 201–3). The event is repeated on 19 September which is the village patronal festival.

Trinity Sunday

Trinity Sunday is the first Sunday after Pentecost and celebrates the doctrine of the Trinity. The day became popular in England probably because St Thomas à Becket was consecrated on that day and actively promoted its use. It formally became a feast day in 1334. Until the sixteenth century, Trinity Sunday was still being celebrated with singing processions followed by feasting in the evening and was also a popular day for wakes. Very few ecclesiastical customs have evolved around this day although a unique instance of rush-strewing took place at the church of Holy Trinity and St. Mary the Virgin, Old Clee in Lincolnshire (Burton 1891: 21). The church was granted a right to cut rushes from a local piece of land, specifically to cover the church floor on Trinity Sunday. However the custom finally disappeared in the 1960s after an accident to one of the parishioners while collecting the reeds.

Charlton-on-Otmoor Garland and Roodscreen. From Parker's Glossary of Architecture, *1840*

Corpus Christi

Corpus Christi (Latin for 'body of Christ') is a feast-day which honours the 'real presence' of Christ's actual body in the consecrated bread or 'Host'. The festival is celebrated on the Thursday after Trinity Sunday. It dates from 1246 and it was instituted after Juliana, a nun near Liege, claimed to have seen a vision denouncing the Church for failing to honour the Eucharist. She claimed to have seen a full, bright moon with one single dark spot which, Christ informed her, represented the lack of a feast for this purpose. The feast was extended to the whole Church in 1264 and by the fifteenth century it had become the chief festival of the Western Church. The feast was suppressed by Protestant Reformers when the doctrine of transubstantiation (maintaining the 'real presence' of Christ in the Eucharist) was rejected. In services the consecrated host is paraded and spectacular processions are still a prominent feature in some parishes (see photograph overleaf). During the last hundred years the Roman Catholic Church have celebrated the day with

A Corpus Christi Procession, Church of Christ the Saviour, Ealing, London, 2008. Photograph by Diocese of London.

a magnificent Carpet of Flowers up the central aisle of Arundel Cathedral in West Sussex and a Procession of the Blessed Sacrament to the nearby Castle. Corpus Christi was particularly noted in the medieval period for miracle plays which were based on cycles of biblical themes and performed by the trade guilds – see Chapter 5.

Pentecost

Pentecost (Greek, meaning 'the Fiftieth Day') commemorates the descent of the Holy Spirit upon the disciples of Christ as described in the Acts of the Apostles (Acts 2). The feast is also called Whit Sunday, Whitsun or Whit, especially in the British Isles. The liturgical colour is red, symbolizing joy and the fire of the Holy Spirit. Traditionally, worshippers wore white clothes on this day but more recently the custom has extended to wearing red clothing.

In addition to the regular Sunday worship, open-air Pentecost services were once very common and are still held on village greens across the country. Baptisms have always been popular on this day and the origin of the name 'Whit Sunday' is generally attributed to the white garments formerly worn by those newly baptised. However, it has also been suggested that the name is a reference to the fresh water consecrated in fonts or may even refer to an old Whitsun custom of rich families giving all the milk of their cows to the poor (Wright and Lones 1936: 148–9). Processions of witness were also common at Whitsun – see Chapter 6.

Many medieval churches throughout Western Europe had a 'Holy Ghost hole' – a small circular opening in the roof and possibly the same feature was used on Ascension Day. At Pentecost these holes would be decorated with flowers and the model of a dove was lowered through into the church while the Pentecost story was read. In old St Paul's Cathedral a live white pigeon was allowed to fly out of the opening (Walcott 1872: 195). A rare example of a Holy Ghost hole can still be seen in Canterbury Cathedral.

Harvest

Harvest Festival used to be celebrated at the beginning of the harvest season on 1 August and was called Lammas (Old English *hlafmaesse*, meaning 'loaf mass') and was regarded as an occasion to give thanks for the first fruits. Farmers made loaves of bread from the new wheat crop and took them to their local church to be blessed for use at a special Communion service thanking God for the harvest. The custom ended with the reformations of Henry VIII although Lammas services are still held in some churches, especially in Devon. It has also been suggested that Lammas originated from the Lamb Mass held in pre-Reformation times on 1 August at the Cathedral of St Peter in Vinculis in York when a lamb was offered during the service (Spicer 1954: 103).

The Harvest is now celebrated at the end of the season with a meal called a Harvest Supper. The modern tradition of celebrating Harvest Festival in churches began in 1843 when the eccentric Reverend Robert Hawker invited parishioners to a special thanksgiving service for the harvest at his church at Morwenstow in Cornwall. Victorian hymns such as 'We plough the fields and scatter', 'Come ye thankful people, come' and 'All things bright and beautiful' promoted his idea of harvest celebration. Many churches throughout the country copied the format of this thanksgiving services and they gradually became known as Harvest Festivals. Nowadays, the food is usually distributed afterwards among the needy of the local community, or used to raise funds for the church or charity. Churches are decorated with a variety of natural produce. Some may include sheaves of wheat, woven straw cones known as 'horns of plenty' and ornate harvest loaves. Occasionally, harvest services have taken place in other communal venues such as the local inn, which was the custom at Rowarth, Derbyshire in the 1950s.

Displaying harvest loaves. Photograph from the Church Times *archive.*

Some local customs have developed around Harvest Festival, such as the hanging of a corn dolly at St Faith's Church, Overbury near Evesham (Day 1999: 127). A famous display of harvest corn dollies can be seen at All Saints church, Siddington in Cheshire every October, where they remain for about a month after the Harvest service. The London Pearly Kings' and Queens' Society hold their own Costermongers' Harvest Festival Parade Service at St Mary-le-Bow church in the City of London. This is preceded by a spectacular street procession of donkeys, carts, marching bands and the distinctive Pearlies themselves. The many outdoor harvest blessing ceremonies are discussed in Chapter 5.

All Saints' Day and All Souls' Day

This festival also known as All Hallows' or Hallowmas ('hallow' from Old English meaning 'holy man') commemorates all the saints. It was originally celebrated on 13 May after its introduction by St Boniface in the seventh century, but Pope Gregory III changed its date to 1 November in the following century. In the Western church it is the day before All Souls' Day

The Rev T. Leslie Weatherhead with the New Mills Parish Choir holds the Harvest Festival Service behind the bar of the Little Mill Inn, Rowarth, Derbyshire. Photograph from the Church Times *archive.*

although in the secular calendar there has been little distinction between the two days. Few national customs seem to be associated with this day although in Derbyshire it was traditional to scatter flowers on the graves of one's relations and friends (Addy 1895a: 125–6).

All Souls' Day was a later addition to the calendar, celebrated on 2 November. This was one of the holy days most vigorously opposed by the Protestant reformers but now continues as a commemoration of the faithful departed. It entered the formal Church calendar in the tenth century and was instituted by St Odilo of Cluny. According to legend, he was persuaded by a pilgrim returning from the Holy Land that on a particular island the plaintive moans of souls in Purgatory could be heard, begging for prayers to release them. It became the duty of all Christians to assist these souls with prayers and acts of charity. On All Souls' Day it was the custom for 'soulers' to attend a church service and then to go around the parish begging for hot 'soulmas' cakes in exchange for reciting prayers for the dead (Black 1981: 60). The modern All Souls' service is, by contrast, a solemn occasion in which the

The annual display of corn dollies at All Saints church, Siddington in Cheshire. Photograph by Averil Shepherd.

names of the deceased members of the parish may be read out. Vigils were held in church, and torch-lit processions took place at dusk. Loud peals were also rung in the belief that this would help their release from Purgatory. In the pre-Reformation period it was also the custom to decorate gravestones and leave offerings of food for hungry returning spirits. The festival has now become intertwined with the modern Hallowe'en celebrations with its playful references to witchcraft and ghosts. This commemorative season includes Remembrance Sunday, which is always the Sunday nearest 11 November (Armistice Day). This day and other commemorative observances are discussed in Chapter 4.

Chapter Seven

Birth:

Rites, Customs and Beliefs

Within the weekly seasonal round of ritual observances and festivals there are the life-cycle offices of baptisms, weddings and funerals which, as David Cressy asserts: 'served as primary points of contact between family and community, centre and periphery, and between men and women and God. Their rhythms and messages were made familiar through frequent reiteration' (Cressy 1993: 106). For Christians this is still the case. In the last three chapters we look at the rites and customs that sustained the cycles of birth, marriage and death.

Birth

Birth like death, is one of the great dramas of the human life-cycle. It is a point of transition that has always demanded some system by which it can be socially legitimised. There is also a complementary need to ritually confirm the spiritual significance of the individual within the family and the wider living community (Clark 1982: 110). The Church has always recognised the fragility of new life and the Book of Common Prayer describes childbirth poignantly as 'a time of great pain and peril'. Every birth is accompanied by a sense of wonder but in the past this has always been tempered by an urgent concern for the child's immediate welfare and survival. Both mother and child are weak and vulnerable, so the hours, days and weeks immediately following childbirth are critical.

In the medieval period these anxieties would have been borne out by the fact that child mortality was a frequent occurrence. Infants often died during labour or within days after birth from infections and illnesses that were poorly understood and for which no cures were available. Survival rates were extremely low. In one London parish early in the reign of Elizabeth I, almost all baptised babies died within a year and around one in forty childbirths resulted in the mother's death (Houlbrooke 1995: 133, 129). However, families were not just preoccupied with medical concerns, for there were powerful beliefs in unwanted supernatural intervention from witches, faeries or other unseen hostile forces that posed an even greater threat to mother and child.

Families with a newborn baby would have placed great confidence in the invocation of positive supernatural forces to ensure a healthy and prosperous life. These protective measures began even before the child was born and the belief that a pregnant mother should eschew certain activities which might affect the future or physical appearance of the unborn child was widespread. Walking while pregnant could be particularly hazardous. In Wales, for example, it was believed that a mother walking outdoors should take care not to walk or step over a grave or her child would die (Trevelyan 1909: 206). Physical deformity was always a possibility, exemplified in the common belief that for a hare to cross the path of a pregnant woman might cause the baby to develop a harelip (Burne 1883: 212–3). Friends and family members were also asked not to alarm expectant mothers through sudden shocks or exposure to animals, which might cause birthmarks to form on the child, in the shape of the agency that caused the fright (Bonham-Carter 1940: 117). Life for an expectant mother was highly restrictive and many other variations of these superstitions were known elsewhere. In a more diminished way, many similar pre-natal safeguards and taboos are probably still tacitly observed today on the principle of 'just in case'.

The rite of baptism

In popular religion, the purpose of baptism was twofold. On the one hand, the rite could obtain enduring security from evil influences and ensure the child's wellbeing. Conversely, if the child had the misfortune to die, then baptism could guarantee its protection in the afterlife. Therefore in uncertain times the event was held as soon as possible. Before the Reformation, it was usual practice to baptise the child on the day of its birth. This was in part a protective measure but could also helpfully facilitate a local astrologer in 'casting the nativity' or telling the fortune of the infant if the family desired it. The fear that prior to the baptism, a child could be spirited away by faeries or receive unwarranted attention from evil spirits was taken very seriously in pre-modern times. So, in the first uncertain hours and days of a new life, precedence was given to observing a vast number of ritual actions to protect both mother and child. Various charms were used as an offensive against such evil threats; salt, a traditional symbol of purity, was believed to be particularly effective for warding off malevolent spirits; garlic, iron objects or a bible hidden under bedclothes in the cradle were also considered to be efficacious. Incantations might also have been employed all with the sole intention of keeping evil forces at bay until a christening could be performed at the earliest possible date in order to obtain ensure the child's long-term physical health. The child was not allowed out of the house before baptism because this could result in illness or a premature death. Equally, it was unthinkable in Yorkshire and elsewhere, well into the nineteenth century, to allow an unbaptised child into a neighbour's house (Clark 1982: 116).

Because the foetus has been traditionally believed to be animated by a human soul from the very beginning of its conception, a weak baby in immediate danger of dying would have been baptised as a matter of urgency. In the Middle Ages, a child who had not been baptised could not receive a Christian burial and its immortal soul was considered to be condemned to eternal damnation. Baptism could not legally be administered to infants unless they showed signs of life, so the greatest anxiety was reserved for stillborn babies or those infants who died during the birth process. An extraordinary range of procedures were used to attempt a temporary revival, including massage, holding the baby upside-down, breathing or pouring wine into its mouth, bathing in various aromatic preparations, or using alternate applications of hot and cold water (Wilson 2000: 226). These were all applied with frantic desperation and it is possible that in some cases a genuine and lasting resuscitation may well have been effected.

Trying to secure the services of a priest, especially in remote rural areas, was not always easy, so in an emergency, a baby could be baptised by the midwife. Indeed, clergy and their curates were charged with ensuring that midwives in their parishes were fully instructed in the appropriate form of words to confer 'conditional baptism'. The correct water was also deemed essential and the midwife was enjoined to use 'pure and clear water only' (Dyer 1891: 111, 112). Lay baptism can still be administered in an emergency to anyone, irrespective of age, who may be in imminent danger of death. It is a simple rite and can be undertaken by a person not normally authorised to administer the sacrament. In early times, especially in the Midlands, this was known as being 'half-baptised', suggesting the expectation that at a later date the child would be fully received into the Church (Palmer 1976: 94).

Baptisms have often been performed privately at home when illness prevailed, but if all was well with both mother and child, a church ritual has always been preferred both by clergy and the family, because it is regarded as a public witness to their faith. However in many communities, baptism was also welcomed as a means of healing infants who were suffering from troublesome ailments. In Lancashire, for example, there was always the hope that a very fractious baby would 'be better' after it had been christened (*Notes and Queries* [1851] 3: 516) while in North Lincolnshire it was reported that an elderly woman believed that a speedy recovery from serious illness would be achieved if a child was baptised at night (*Notes and Queries* [1893] 4: 207). In Shropshire, baptism was also considered to be a cure for convulsions (Burne 1883: 192). Remarkably, this idea of applying baptism as a charm for healing and good fortune has persisted into modern times; even as recently as 1962, an appropriately intolerant headline in the *Daily Express* (15 Nov 1962: 20, quoted by Opie and Tatem 1989: 72) read: 'Vicar says bar baptism for "good luck" babies'.

Baptism and the afterlife

In Christianity, baptism (Greek *baptizo*, 'immersion' or 'performing ablutions') is the central rite of admission into the Church, although is not unique to Christianity and was practised in various forms as an initiation rite by pagan religions. A form of baptismal rite was practised by the Jews for centuries prior to Jesus Christ as an act of spiritual purification. In most Christian traditions, the liturgy of baptism is understood as a process of spiritual cleansing but more importantly, it is viewed literally as symbolic dying, burial and resurrection, so that the individual undergoes an actual supernatural transformation and 'rises with Christ'. In the New Testament, the rite is initiated when Jesus is baptised by John the Baptist (Matt. 3). Although there is no scriptural command for its application to converts to the faith, baptism became and remains the accepted rite of initiation into the Christian faith in most denominations.

Throughout history the need to baptise has always had a doctrinal urgency about it, because in the strictest Christian teaching, unbaptised children could not enter Heaven and there was great concern among the faithful about what happened to their souls after death. The Roman Catholic Church created the speculative idea of Limbo (Latin *limbus*, 'edge' or 'boundary') to explain their future and this was conceived as a painless and possibly liminal state, without any kind of torment or punishment. For centuries, this was officially the post-mortem status of those who died in infancy; they were regarded as too young to have committed personal sins, but tragically, not free from original sin. Thankfully, in 2007, the Catholic Church reconsidered and then withdrew its teaching on Limbo.

Folklore has stepped in to offer many explanations for the afterlife of unbaptised infants and most of these have made a metaphorical link with the natural world, although few of them are particularly reassuring. Their souls were destined to be earth-bound and could return in various forms. There was a widespread belief that they could return as butterflies or moths, or they might also return as Will o' the Wisps. In Devonshire they might become one of the Yeth Hounds hunted with the Devil across Dartmoor (Radford and Radford 1961: 346). Many of these explanations would have deeply troubled medieval minds and only served to underline the imperative of an expedient baptism.

Naming the child

A primary function of baptism in popular culture has always been the act of giving an identity to the child. However, in this respect, there is a good deal of confusion about the words 'christening' and 'baptism'. The term 'to christen' in vernacular language, is often a misnomer because of its muddled use and application. 'Christening' is an old English folkloric word that was, and still is, often used for baptism, but both are identical rites. The word 'christening' now tends to be reserved for the baptism of infants. However, the popular perception of the term 'christening', designates the giving of a 'Christian name' to an individual when, in the strictest sense, it refers to making a person one of Christ's faithful. It literally means 'to bring to Christ'. In a wider folkloric sense, name-giving ceremonies are sometimes referred to as 'secular christenings' although they are without any spiritual validity, and there has of course never been a requirement for any individual to undergo an authentic christening ceremony in order to be considered as truly 'named'.

However, in spite of official definitions, to name a child was formerly considered a powerful act to be undertaken with the greatest care and reverence. Traditionally, in the history of pagan religions, the act of giving a child a name was in itself an important rite of passage. The naming of a child carried considerable spiritual significance, which may possibly explain the lingering populist belief that baptism is primarily a 'naming' ceremony. Within the pre-Reformation Church however, the act of naming was not prioritised in the baptismal rite, but in the 1549 Book of Common Prayer the priest names the child at the signing in the first part of the service. Thereafter, the giving of the 'Christian name' was liturgically invested with a new significance and became an essential part of the rite, although in recent times it has taken on an exaggerated importance. Disclosing the name of the child to anyone but the closest relatives prior to the baptism was considered to be unlucky. Therefore, an occasional safeguard involved writing the name on a piece of paper which was pinned onto the child's christening clothes for the attention of the priest (Bennett 1992: 68). In East Anglia, naming the child was considered by nurses to be essential to its immediate good health (Forby 1830: 406–7) and if the newborn was sickly, this was often a popular argument to justify a hasty private baptism.

Circumstances did not always permit a newborn child to be named with familial care and consideration. In the sixteenth century, infants who were weak and seemed unlikely to live, would be summarily baptised by a midwife with such names as 'Creature', 'Creatura Christi' or 'Children of God'. Parish registers record many examples, and it was not unknown for sickly children to surprise all concerned and go on to live healthy lives and marry with the inevitable ordeal of living with such unendearing names! Many other naming practices are locally recorded. In some parishes it was the custom to name abandoned children, known as 'foundlings', after the parishes in which they were found; so, for example, children found in the precincts of St Clement Danes in the City of London were called Clement, and numerous occurrences of this manner of naming are to be found in parish registers (Dyer 1891: 112; 114). In some areas, bestowing the Christian name of the incumbent of a parish upon the first boy brought to the font after his institution (Tyack 1899: 172) was not unusual. It was also a common practice to name a child after the saint on whose day it had been born (Dyer 1891: 114–15) and, then as now, it was not unusual for families to have a celebration for their child on the designated feast day.

Choosing the godparents

Baptism expressed in spiritual terms is not an end in itself, in spite of popular belief, but a beginning. Consequently, a newly born child needed a godparent who would take on the role of Christian mentor or spiritual guardian. The idea of a godparent or 'sponsor', came about because converts to the early Christian church were usually adults whose parents were not Christians. Over the years it became a supporting role in which other adults agreed to help the parents instruct and inform their new offspring in the Christian faith. This role has been eroded, for many families in the present and the religious significance of a godparent is now less apparent than the honorary status. Others link the role of godparent with that of 'legal guardian' and ask them to take on the responsibility of bringing up the child if he or she is ever to be left orphaned.

Godparents were usually chosen by the parents and have always been charged with the duty of helping raise the child to believe in the Church's commandments as well as to guide him or her as the child grows up. In popular thought, anyone becoming a godparent was endowed with more than qualities of spiritual guidance and they also became invested with healing powers. In Shropshire, for example, a garter or other item belonging to the godmother or godfather was considered a curative artefact and if worn by the infant as a cure for whooping cough (Burne 1883: 192).

A godmother was formerly known as a 'gossip'. By the mid-fourteenth century the word was applied in almost exclusive reference to women, and

The tomb of a chrism-child, St Margaret's Church, Stanford Rivers, Essex. Photograph by Mark Lewis.

by the period 1590–1670 was used to describe selected female friends who were invited to be present at the birth of a child (Warner 1992: 54). A christening feast in former times was consequently known as a 'gossiping'. Subsequently, and partly because of women's involvement in family and communal storytelling, a gossip came to refer to a women who was given to idle chatter. Godmothers always had great importance immediately after the birth of a child, to provide comfort and support to the mother and help in preparation for the baptism.

Preparing for baptism

On the day of the baptism a variety of preparations and safeguards were made even before the family arrived at the church. While the unbaptised child was confined to the house, it was not unusual, even in the twentieth century, for other siblings to be confined to their homes until the baptism of the new arrival had taken place, for fear of misfortune. In the medieval period it was the practice for child on the day of its baptism, to be arrayed by the priest in a white robe to symbolise its purity, which had first been anointed with sacred oil. In more recent times dressing the infant has been

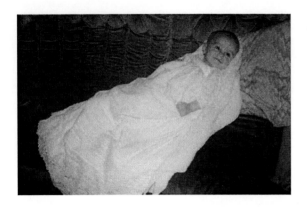

Author's son in a traditional christening robe, 1987. Photograph by Mark Lewis.

undertaken by the mother. A white christening cap was also worn and in Northumberland it was considered essential that this remained on the head of the child for that remainder of the day and night (Henderson 1866: 8).

The robe was called a 'chrisom' or 'chrismale' or sometimes a 'bearing sheet', 'christening sheet' or 'christening palm', and if the child died within a month of its baptism, it was shrouded and buried in this robe and known as a chrism-child (Hole 1953: 139). Dressing the baby in a christening robe is still considered important in contemporary baptismal culture among Christian families of long lineage; many of these garments are cherished family heirlooms, reverently handed down through successive generations.

In Hampshire there was an unusual christening custom among the rural poor which reflects a particularly amiable relationship between parson and parishioner. If the tenth child of a family was born while the others were still alive, it was brought to baptism with a sprig of myrtle in its cap to signify that it was a 'tithe child'. In the early medieval period this child was usually given to the church as a tithe. Evidently the custom was still known even in the early nineteenth century and at that time the Church seems to have taken responsibility for schooling of the infant. Another instance was recorded at Compton in Surrey, but because of high mortality rates, this observance must have been extremely rare (Yonge 1892: 200; Vaux 1894: 75–6).

Once all the preparations were in place the family and friends would usually walk together in procession to the church. A widespread practice en route was to offer a piece of christening cake to the first person they met. A well-established custom in the northern counties was for parents taking a child to baptism to carry a paper bag containing a cheese sandwich, a slice of cake and a silver coin. Sometimes candle and salt were also included; the first person of the sex opposite to that of the child to be seen by the christening party on their way to the church received this curious collection. Sometimes it was also given out at the church gate after the ceremony. The custom was still being observed in the 1970s (*FLS News* 11 1990: 4–7; 12 1991: 10–13).

The water of baptism

The baptism of infants is not specifically mentioned in the New Testament, but the first traces are found in the Western Church after the middle of the second century (Cote 1876: 110) and it became the rule around the twelfth century. Adult immersion, with Jesus' baptism as the prototype, seems to have been the favoured mode in the early Church, performed in the sea, streams or rivers and this form is still used by many Christian communities today. Most Christians now baptise by pouring three times on the forehead, traditionally from a scallop shell, 'in the name of the Father, and of the Son and of the Holy Spirit'.

The baptismal ceremony is literally a form of ritual washing, almost always performed with water as a symbol of life and purity. The most potent and spiritually significant water was brought from the River Jordan where Christ was baptised and this was always used for royal christenings. In the medieval Church, the holy water used in baptism would have been ritually consecrated on Holy Saturday or Whitsun and holy oils mixed with it. Children were sometimes taken to be baptised at holy wells and the water from them was considered to be particularly efficacious because of its healing properties and power to protect a child from evil spirits. During the eighteenth century, many wells that were known to have supplied baptismal water for the church were probably called holy for this reason (Harte 2008: 105). In some cases the baptisms were conducted at the well and the child was fully immersed in the water. Although the usual practice was to baptise a child at the font, a moving exception was recorded in the early nineteenth century in Monmouthshire; when a mother died shortly after child-birth it was the custom for the infant to be baptised on her coffin at the funeral and the ceremony was performed in the church porch (Carrington 1859: 88).

The water blessed and used in baptism was effectively an elixir in popular religion and sought after for its alleged curative powers. Even up to the late Victorian period, priests often received requests from mothers who believed that bathing their children in it would have beneficial effects or they would administer it is a medicine. In the Parish of Churcham, Gloucestershire, it was recorded in the nineteenth century that a nurse invariably used sanctified water remaining after baptism to wash out the mouth of baptised infants as a safeguard against toothache (*Notes and Queries* [1874] I: 383). Water from holy wells which had been used at a baptism was considered effective for sore eyes and in Somerset, the water from the font was also believed to be good for ague and rheumatism (Vaux 1894: 279; *Notes and Queries* [1854] 9: 536).

Casting out the Devil

During the Middle Ages, the imperative action in the rite of baptism was to cast out the Devil from the child and this was regarded with utmost seriousness. A baptismal ceremony was to all intents and purposes an exorcism, and a vestige of this character still remains within the ritual. In spite of the extensive precautions taken to protect the newly-born child from evil influences, there was still clearly an assumption that the Devil had already laid claim to the infant and had to be ritually ejected from the body. Indeed, in the early centuries of the church, it was customary to exorcise adult converts prior to their receiving baptism. This rite of exorcism, which at first only called upon the candidates to 'renounce the Devil and all his works', was eventually modified to include certain prayers in the name of Christ, which commanded the Devil to quit the persons about to be baptised.

There was a widespread belief that the north of the church was the province of the Devil. This explains why many unbaptised children were buried in that 'heathen' area of the graveyard. There may be an association between pagan religion and the north doors by which the pagan population entered the church, many of which are considered to have been built on former pagan sites. North doors of very small dimensions, known simply as 'Devil doors', appeared in many medieval churches in the British Isles. Although they are occasionally recorded as being opened for the passage of funerals (Lambourn 1912: 188) they were never really intended for human use. These doors were kept ajar during baptisms, to allow the exit of the Devil from the child, who might otherwise potentially meet and enter into someone coming in by the usual door nearer the south or west sides of the building. It is also known that these doors were sometimes opened during the ritual of exorcism, for the same purpose. Most of these doorways were been bricked up in the post-Reformation period, supposedly to deter the Devil from re-entering the church (Collins 2007: 52), although an increasing recognition of their superstitious use probably hastened their removal. Surviving examples of Devil doors can still be found in many British Churches, with a notable concentration in Sussex.

Ritual superstitions and baptismal eccentricities

The ceremony of baptism has always been enshrouded with a variety of superstitious beliefs and practices from earliest times. The first child baptised in a new church was believed to be claimed by the Devil, a remnant of an ancient belief the first living thing to enter a new sacred building was given

A Saxon Devil Door at the church of St Giles, Horsted Keynes, West Sussex. Photograph by Mark Lewis.

up to the Devil (Radford and Radford 1949:72). It was considered essential for a child to cry at baptism as this was believed to be the voice of the evil spirit being driven out by the power of the holy water (Radford and Radford 1949:27), and this understanding probably evolved from the custom of exorcism, for the Devil was always believed to leave the possessed infant with great reluctance. Copious tears and physical struggles were therefore regarded as a healthy sign that the Devil was departing the child. A family would be particularly alarmed if a child was quiet during the ritual so midwives or officiating clergy were often known to pinch the infant to make it cry. Indeed, if a child that did not cry during the ceremony, this was a worrying sign that it would probably be short-lived (Grose 1787: 51).

If girls and boys were to be baptised together, then it was essential that a correct order was followed. In the north of England, baptism was always to be administered to a boy before a girl (Henderson 1879: 16). If this sequence was not followed a boy would be condemned to go through adult life with a smooth and beardless face while the girl would have to contend with a heavy growth of facial hair! After the baptism, the child was handed to one of the godparents and anointed on the head with the chrism accompanied by an appropriate prayer. The ceremony concluded by the priest reciting passages from the New Testament over the child, including the story relating the exorcism of the demoniac boy in Mark's Gospel (Mark 9: 26). This last reading was deemed to be particularly important in finally ensuring the expulsion of the Devil.

In spite of belief in the infallible spiritual and power of the official rite, some communities felt the need to supplement this with other superstitious forms of baptism. Even animals were baptised and numerous cases of attempts to baptise cats, dogs, sheep and horses were recorded in the sixteenth and seventeenth centuries. Some of these instances were undoubtedly a mockery by Puritans setting out to denounce Anglican ceremonial, but they may also have been informed by an earlier superstition that the baptismal rite had physical virtues which could be bestowed upon any living creature (Thomas 1997: 37). The name 'baptism' was sometimes applied improperly to other ceremonies such as the blessing of bells, which were ritually anointed with holy water (Fanning 1907), and ships were also blessed and 'baptised' to protect all who sailed in them. A vestige of this latter ceremonial remains in the launching of a new vessel by breaking a bottle of champagne against its bow.

The churching of women

The safe delivery of the infant and its expedient baptism was certainly not the end of the protracted social and religious activities for the mother. After the birth, the mother would remain at home in seclusion; she could not reconnect with community life until she had undergone the ritual known as 'churching'. Vernacular names for the ceremony are rare but in Devonshire, it was sometimes curiously referred to as 'being uprose' (Vaux 1894: 87). Churching has always been surrounded by controversy, because of the historical tension between the understanding of the rite as a form of cleansing for women who are seen as defiled by giving birth on one hand, and a ceremony of thanksgiving for the safe birth of a child on the other. The ritual evolved from Jewish ideas of ritual impurity and the need for purification after childbirth (Leviticus 12), which passed into the mainstream practices of the Christian Church. The rite eventually came to be seen as an obligation by the English church and its most recent form probably dates from the eleventh century. The 1549 Book of Common Prayer called it 'The Order of Purification of Women', which made it clear that the mother, in her immediate post-natal state, harboured malevolent spirits and was therefore unclean.

However, as David Cressy has observed, like many rituals, churching in its outward form could conceal a variety of meanings (Cressy 1993: 111). Many women regarded churching as a social necessity as much as a religious requirement in both Protestant and Catholic churches; it has been aptly described as 'the social return from childbirth' (van Gennep 1960: 46). In some areas of Wales, women must have regarded the prospect of the ceremony with a good measure of enthusiasm, because it was reported that the ritual was thought to be effective as a charm against witchcraft (Kittredge 1929: 145) – a belief which was probably held more widely. However, the later rite developed with greater conviction as a ceremony of thanksgiving and even into the late twentieth century, when churching went out of favour, many women, willingly attended a ceremony to give thanks for the safe delivery of their children. Indeed, the modern church offers a formal liturgy of thanksgiving precisely for this very purpose, but divested of any notions of a purification rite.

The confinement of the mother before her churching was observed with utmost seriousness. Inevitably, the woman's seclusion and the whole churching process acquired a superstitious significance. An unchurched woman who dared to leave her home risked misfortune or social rejection. Any attempt to visit a neighbour's home could be met with stout physical resistance so the day of the churching ritual would have been greeted with considerable relief. The ceremony began with the woman kneeling at the church door, 'decently apparelled', according to the rubric in the Prayer Book, and wearing a veil. She would be directed to sit in a special 'churching' or 'church-wife' pew, sometimes carrying a lighted taper as an allusion to the feast of Candlemas.

In Herefordshire, and in other areas, attendance of the husband was frowned upon, but if he insisted on doing so, he would sit in a pew at some distance behind his wife (Vaux 1894: 87). The officiating midwife may also have been present, and accommodated in a 'midwife pew' a short distance behind her. The woman to be churched would sit while the priest read prayers from the 'reading pew' (Addleshaw and Etchells 1948: 84). At the end of the ritual, the woman might take Holy Communion and make some offering to the church, such as the chrisom which had enshrouded her baptised infant. She was now ready to take her place once again in the social order of the community.

Coming of age and confirmation

The rite of passage that follows baptism is that of confirmation and this ceremony has always been seen as sealing the covenant made in the baptismal rite. The ritual has Biblical authority (Acts 8:14–17) and the earliest attestation of the ceremony, dates from AD 215. A child as young as twelve months could be confirmed in the thirteenth century but seven years of age gradually became the minimum age for candidates (Thomas 1997: 37) at which point it was considered that they could make a reasonably mature commitment to their faith. The rite can only be performed by a bishop and in

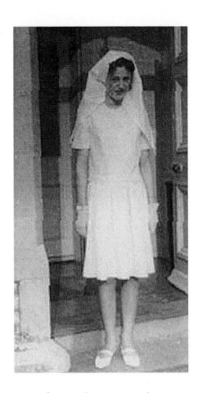

The author's wife in confirmation dress, 1965. Photograph by Rev D.A.P. Shiels.

popular culture, confirmation was often known as 'bishopping'. It is still regarded by many denominations as a coming of age ceremony but is essentially intended to 'confirm' or 'strengthen' the candidate in his or her life of faith.

It was customary for a girl presenting herself for confirmation to wear a simple white dress and although these are still part of the traditional dress code for Catholics, their use has now faded away in the Anglican Church. During the crucial element of the confirmation rite those to be confirmed renew their baptismal promises; the bishop places his hands over the head of the candidate for the purpose of bestowing the Gift of the Holy Spirit. This is followed by anointing them with oil on the forehead, the imposition of the hand on the head of each and making the sign of the cross on the forehead. Confirmation is normally followed straight away by Holy Communion. There is an interesting footnote to the ritual as it was practised in the medieval period when, after anointing with oil, the confirmed person's head was bound with a white headband which had to be worn for several days. Confirmed children would then return to the church where their foreheads were washed near the font, after which the headbands were gathered together and burnt. This was undertaken out of a superstitious reverence for the hallowed oil (Tyack 1899: 176).

The laying on of hands in the confirmation rite is particularly important because the act of touching involves affirmation, identification and love. Curiously, only a few superstitious customs have attached themselves to this ritual, probably because in popular Christianity, all that needs to be conferred upon a young person to ensure well-being, was believed to have been achieved at baptism. Confirmation, like baptism is a permanent sacrament and only needs to be undertaken once, although this clearly did not stop people putting themselves forward again, particularly as there was a common belief that the rite acted as a form of restorative tonic that was particularly good for rheumatic complaints. Robert Forby (Forby 1830: 406–7) reports an elderly woman in East Anglia who presented herself for confirmation, remarking that she 'had been bishopped seven times, and intended to again, because it was so good for her rheumatism'. E.M. Leather describes a woman in Herefordshire who sought the same cure and obviously managed to escape recognition by being confirmed in three different churches! (Leather 1912: 80). The touch of a senior cleric was no doubt thought to contribute to the potency of the charm although it would fail to work if the bishop touched the candidate with his right hand (Radford and Radford 1949: 85).

Chapter Eight

Marriage:

Wedding Customs and Beliefs

Marriage is the oldest institution of society and another of life's great transitional moments. In the eleventh century, marriage was declared to be a sacrament and during the Reformation it was further affirmed as an institution of God. Nonetheless, in spite of its sacred status, prior to the Council of Trent in the mid-sixteenth century, a valid marriage in the eyes of the Church could be accomplished by a simple declaration of the betrothed parties to be man and wife; no priest or witnesses were required and inevitably this was open to considerable abuse (Andrews 1895: 100). True marriage however, has always required commitment and responsibility, so numerous customs have developed around the wedding rituals in every culture in order to protect and sustain the couple. Most marriage celebrations, whether they are Christian or secular, still retain many folkloric elements that have stood the test of time. Here we explore the nuptial customs that take place under ecclesiastical authority and within the precincts of the church.

Fertility rites and nuptial contracts

Throughout history, wedding rites and the feasting that follows them have always been considered to be conducive to promoting fertility. Promoting child-bearing has certainly been endorsed in Christian ritual and the Book of Common Prayer called for God's blessing 'on these two persons, that they may both be 'fruitful in procreation of children'. In medieval Europe there was further approval expressed in the custom of the priest blessing the marriage bed. The couple, the bed and others present were blessed with incense, sprinkled with holy water and official prayers of protection and sanctification were offered. There was always a strong element of protective magic in these fertility rituals and throughout Europe all kinds of rites were performed to safeguard bridal couples from the harmful influences of evil spirits. Some of these, as we will see, still remain in modern celebrations.

The timing of a wedding has always been important and in pre-Reformation times this was strictly regulated. The Church prohibited marriages taking place from Advent Sunday until the octave of the Epiphany (St Hilary's Day, 13 January); from Septuagesima (the ninth Sunday before Easter) until the octave of Easter (Easter Sunday) and from Rogation Sunday until six days after Pentecost (Vaux 1894: 90–1). Special licences were required to be married at any other time. A piece of doggerel from a church register at Everton, Nottinghamshire (Andrews 1890: 154) clearly states the situation:

> Advent marriage doth deny,
> But Hilary gives thee liberty;
> Septuagesima says thee nay;
> Eight days from Easter says you may;
> Rogation bids thee to contain,
> But Trinity sets thee free again.

The above appears to have been a popular verse and with minor variations, it is to be found in several parishes registers. These regulated periods were clearly taken very seriously and bishops and archdeacons making their visitations in the seventeenth century were in the habit of inquiring whether any persons had unlawfully married during the proscribed periods.

Calling the Banns

After betrothal and engagement there is a series of legal pronouncements made within the Church. These announcements are known as the 'banns of marriage', (Middle English *bannan* 'to summon or proclaim' from which also comes the word 'banner'). This is the public announcement of an impending marriage between two specified persons. A marriage was only legally valid if the banns had been called or a marriage licence had been obtained. This very ancient custom dates back to the twelfth century (Vaux 1894: 91) and continues today, although the Roman Catholic Church abolished the requirement in 1983. However, during the Commonwealth period in Britain (1649–60), marriage was considered to be merely a civil contract; banns were published in the secular market-place and the marriage ceremony was performed by a Justice of the Peace (Ditchfield 1907: 81).

The main purpose of 'calling the banns' is to enable anyone to raise a legal impediment to the marriage, and thereby prevent an invalid union. These legal barriers might include a pre-existing marriage that has not been dissolved or annulled, a lack of consent, a vow of celibacy, or a close blood relationship between the couple. The banns were regarded as binding and a couple who suddenly changed their minds after these announcements were said to have 'mocked the church' and could be fined. For example, it was the custom at Norham, Durham, up to the nineteenth century that if the banns were published twice and the marriage did not take place, one of the dissenting couple had to pay forty shillings to the vicar for 'scorning the Church' (Vaux 1894: 94). A couple refusing to marry could also suffer serious local disapproval and even be ostracised by their community.

The banns were required to be read aloud on three Sundays before the wedding ceremony, in the home parish churches of both parties. Traditionally they were delivered from the pulpit and the Church of England wording always begins: 'I publish the banns of marriage between nn of … and nn of …' Until the late nineteenth century it was not unusual in some areas after the calling for the Parish Clerk, or the whole congregation to be charged to say in congratulatory tones, 'God speed them well'. After the banns had been read and if no challenges had been made, it was customary in certain parishes in Nottinghamshire after the first 'asking' for a 'banns peal' or 'spurring peal' (from *spier*, to ask) to be rung to bring a blessing on the couple (Ingram 1954: 76).

The calling of banns was often generally known as 'asking', 'shouting', 'spurring' or 'calling home' (Monger 2004: 19). However, there were also many regional variants. In East Lincolnshire a couple whose marriage banns had been proclaimed three times in church were said to be 'axed-up' or 'axed-out' (Good 1906: 16). In Yorkshire, a couple having their having banns called were said to be 'hanging in the bell ropes' (Blakeborough 1898: 95) while in Sussex it was referred to as being 'church-cried' or 'bawled' (Parish 1875: 27). In York and Pembrokeshire it was known as 'falling over the pulpit' (Tyack 1999: 179).

Because of the hostile supernatural forces that were believed to hang over a betrothed couple, a number of superstitions evolved around the timing and calling of the banns. In Lincolnshire, if the bell was tolled for the death of a married woman on the same day that the banns were called for the third and last time it would presage that the new bride would live longer than the first year of her married life (Monger 2004: 19). A superstition from Lancashire and Yorkshire states that if a person – usually a woman – goes to church to hear their banns called, their children will be born deaf and dumb. Incredibly, this was reported to have prevailed in Sussex as recently as 1942 (Harland and Wilkinson 1873: 222; Opie and Tatum 1989: 239)

A Fleet wedding.

Fleet marriages

The calling of banns became a particularly serious issue after 1753 when Lord Hardwicke's Marriage Act came into force. This was the first statutory regulation in England and Wales to require a formal ceremony of marriage and was primarily aimed at putting a stop to the many clandestine marriages that were taking place. Before this date, many Anglican clergymen were flouting ecclesiastical rules and covertly marrying couples without the publication of banns. Most of these clerics were penniless and unscrupulous prisoners in the Fleet debtors' prison in London, who were prepared to celebrate irregular marriages for a reasonable gratuity, without asking awkward questions. These 'Fleet parsons' conducted their trade in the many nearby 'marriage houses' or local taverns where landlords willingly engaged touts or 'plyers' to seek custom for the clerics. There were also a number of unprincipled clerks who augmented their earnings by recording the marriages. The first of these illicit ceremonies took place in 1674 and many people then took advantage of 'the Liberty of the Fleet' (Ashton 1888: 331–3). These marriages were sought after by a variety of desperate and tragic figures, including drunkards, fortune hunters, society ladies saddled with heavy debts, and spinsters in search of a husband. When the navy was docked in the Port of London, it was not unusual for around three hundred sailors to seek a 'Fleet Marriage' (Baker 1977: 47).

The Marriage Act required banns to be published and the marriage to be solemnised in church. Thereafter, any clergyman who dared to conduct an illegal marriage was liable to transportation. This new legal requirement meant that elopers had to leave England and Wales in order to contract a marriage by evading the formalities. Gretna Green, in Dumfrieshire Scotland, was the customary destination for many runaway couples, owing to a loophole in old Scottish law which required only an acknowledgement before witnesses in order to constitute a valid marriage. The ceremony took place in an old blacksmith's shop; the local blacksmiths performed the rite and eventually became known as 'anvil priests'. These 'runaway marriages' continued until the Marriage Act of 1856 required the couple to be resident for twenty-one days in the parish where the marriage was to take place and 'Gretna' marriages became invalid. However, civil and religious marriages still take place at Gretna Green although legally administered through the jurisdiction of a local registrar's office.

Smock weddings

One of the great curiosities of nuptial folklore is the 'smock wedding'. This derived from the popular notion that a man is not liable for his wife's debts if she wears only her shift or smock when she marries him. The bride would arrive barefoot at the church, sometimes stripping to her shift within the church door before proceeding to the altar. There is another variation of this belief in which the same freedom from financial obligations could be obtained if the bride walked from her own home to that of her husband. The underlying motivation for this custom seems to be that a woman would symbolically shed her debts with her clothes. Therefore by coming to her married life wearing nothing, there could be no transference of her previous debts to her future husband. An early law states that the responsibility of the husband for his wife's pre-nuptial debts depended on the extent of the fortune she had brought him. A smock wedding served as public notice that his bride brought nothing to the marriage and therefore no claims could be made against him for her past obligations (Mikkelson 2005).

The wedding day

On the wedding day, the bride and groom are supported by their attendants and collectively they form the 'bridal party'. This dates back to Anglo-Saxon days when the groom would literally go out to 'capture' his bride, and needed the help of his friends who became known as the 'bride's men' or 'bride knights'. They would also make sure the bride got to the church and to the groom's house afterwards. This is the origin of the modern role that we refer to as 'best man'. At an Anglo-Saxon wedding the bride was led to the church by a matron, who was called the 'bride's woman', and followed by a company of young girls who were called 'bridesmaids'. It became popular for children to be given the role of bridesmaid and they were included in the ceremonial procession to confirm notions of purity and innocence. In the pre-modern period it was the custom for the bridesmaids to lead the bridegroom to the church, and for the bridegroom's men to conduct the bride (Andrews 1895: 103). Anglo-Saxon England was often an unpredictable and violent place and grooms often had to defend their brides, so it became customary for the bride to stand to the left of her groom in church so that his sword arm was free.

Both bride and groom dress in special clothing that will make them stand out and prepare themselves for public ceremonial that is designed to fix the event in the memory of all concerned. However, the bride is the centre of attention on the day and white has always been the favoured colour for her dress. The colour signifies purity but, in older traditions, it was also believed to deter the evil eye (Baker 1977: 68). The tradition that a bride should wear a veil on her wedding day may well have been used as a similar protective measure although it was primarily intended to symbolise her modesty and virginity. Head adornment was also popular and in many churches it was usual to keep a crown of metal for the use of brides, and for which they would pay a fee (Andrews 1895: 105–6). Other ornaments such as jewellery and even the bridal veil were sometimes provided by the parish on a similar basis (Gasquet 1906: 210).

Flowers were incorporated into the ceremony because of their rich symbolism including representations of fertility, purity, new life and eternal love. Traditionally, bouquets were always a mixture of flowers and herbs, with orange blossom favoured to confer fertility. It was an ancient belief throughout Europe that strong smelling herbs, garlic or spices would drive away evil spirits and ill health so brides would carry them for this purpose. At an Anglo-Saxon wedding, after the benediction in the church, both the bride and bridegroom were crowned with flowers. Wreaths made of ears of corn were frequently worn by brides in the time of Henry VIII and myrtle was also much used for the same purpose. Curiously, rosemary, which was more commonly used as a plant at funerals, was also worn at weddings as a 'remembrance against sorcery' and the sprigs were often gilded or dipped in scented water (Baker 1977: 88; Andrews 1895: 107).

Arriving at the church

It was a common practice up to the nineteenth century for many bridal parties to walk to church on foot. Therefore, the route of the wedding procession and the church itself received some special preparation in some areas. In Monkswearmouth, Sunderland during the nineteenth century, the road by which a wedding procession was to go to church was sometimes strewn with sawdust. This was only done for a marriage in church and it was locally known as a 'sawdust wedding' (*Notes and Queries* [1876] 5: 186). A more complex and unique custom at Knutsford, Cheshire involved 'sanding' the bride's path to church with decorative patterns including the words 'long life and happiness' (Baker 1977: 88). Until the eighteenth century it was customary to decorate the church for weddings and in Shropshire the floors were often garlanded with flowers.

The timing of arrival at the church could be an issue and it was not unusual for weddings and funerals to happen at the same time within the precincts of the same building. In this situation it was considered very unlucky for a wedding party to meet a funeral and some churchyards were supplied with two gates for use by the different processions – see also Chapter 9. In many parishes it was also considered prudent to circle the church three times in a sunwise direction before entering the building (Baker 1974: 141). Sometimes on arrival at the churchyard gate other local traditions of decoration would have been observed, such as the unique custom described by Augustus Hare, which greeted him at his own wedding at Stoke-upon-Tern, Shropshire in 1829 (Hare 1872: 245). All of the silver spoons, tankards, watches and ornaments of the neighbouring farmers were fastened on white cloths drawn over hoops and displayed on each side of the churchyard gate. It was suggested that the trinkets were probably a form of charm by which to bestow prosperity and good fortune on the bridal couple as they passed through the gate. The custom is believed to have continued until at least 1840 (Tyack 1999: 68).

The wedding ceremony

A wedding ceremony is a very public event in which promises are made before a community of witnesses. Two people are giving themselves in love but the ritual also involves visible symbols of giving and acceptance, which traditionally provide assurances between the two families. In pre-modern times a daughter was considered to be the property of the father and he had the right to give his child to the groom, but usually for financial gain. A vestige of this custom survives in the modern ceremony although a father will now 'give away' his daughter to express his blessing of the marriage. The contract is expected to be binding and it is still customary in many churches for the priest to wrap the ends of his stole around the joined hands of the bride and bridegroom, at the words 'Those whom God has joined together...' symbolising an indissoluble union. It is has been suggested that this practice led to the familiar expression 'tying the knot' (Andrews 1895: 101).

During the medieval period, the nuptial rite was divided into two distinct ceremonies. The first part was a secular contract known as the *sponsalia* in which the couple gave their full assent to the contract of marriage. This involved the bridegroom giving the ring to the bride (the *subarrhatio*) and the promise of a dowry before a gathering of witnesses. The second part was the sacramental and spiritual element known as the *matrimonium,* which consisted of the couple receiving Holy Communion and a blessing. During the benediction, a veil or 'care-cloth' was suspended over them, usually held at its four corners by as many clerics. In the last part of the ceremony, the priest would turn himself towards the married couple and gave them the nuptial blessing. The cloth was then removed, and the bridegroom received the 'kiss of peace' from the priest; he then turned to his bride and kissed her upon the cheek (Monger 2004: 60). The modern ceremony has lost many of these elements but still retains a strong sacramental liturgy concluding with the nuptial blessing.

However, before the Reformation it was usual for the contractual part of the ritual – the *sponsalia* – to take place at the door of the church. Therefore, one practical reason why the south porch of many churches was built to large dimensions was to accommodate the wedding party. The bride and groom would be met by the priest at the porch and the ring would be blessed and hallowed. After this ceremony the priest recited a benediction over the couple and led them into the church to the first step before the altar for the mass and a final solemn nuptial blessing (Gasquet 1906: 209; Postles 2007: 755–6). There were clearly local variations of this practice and at Witham, Essex, for example it was the custom to perform the first part of the marriage service at the font (Vaux 1894: 98). It was not until the sixteenth century in England, that weddings were allowed to be performed entirely within the church.

The wedding ring

In the Anglo-Saxon period, it was customary to use a ring as means to pledge betrothal, similar to the concept of the engagement ring; it was placed on the woman's right hand, where it remained until the marriage ceremony when it was transferred to the left (Andrews 1895: 107). The ring came to represent a promise of eternal and everlasting love and has been an official part of the Christian wedding ceremony since the seventh century. The ritual blessing of the ring and the act of putting it on the bride's finger dates from the eleventh century. Traditionally, it has always been placed on the open prayer book of the officiating priest. An additional custom which only seems to have been recorded in the north of England, required the bridegroom to place on the book a 'dow purse' alongside the ring; this was supposed to represent 'all his worldly goods' and visibly demonstrate that all he possessed was to be shared with his wife (Vaux 1894: 99).

The ring is a representation of the promises joining both the bride and groom together and is traditionally worn on the fourth finger of the left hand. This ruling was specified in the 1549 Book of Common Prayer, although during the reigns of George I and George II, the wedding ring was often worn on the thumb (Andrews 1895: 107). The fourth finger tradition probably derives from the Roman belief that the vein in this finger was directly connected to the heart and therefore the obvious place to display a symbol representing eternal love and commitment. It was customary in medieval Europe, to ceremonially place the ring in sequence on the index, middle, and ring fingers of the left hand. The ring was then left on the ring finger. According to the Sarum Use, this practice is explained by the bridegroom putting the ring on the first finger of the bride saying: 'in the name of the Father (on the first finger) and of the Son (on the third finger) and of the Holy Ghost (the third finger)' with the injunction that it should be left there (Baker 1977: 76). Baring-Gould however, went further and took a survivalist view by suggesting that putting the finger through a ring is probably a vestige of the ancient practice of passing the entire body through a ring of stone as a symbol of covenant, and implying that the bride is being regenerated by entering a new family (Baring-Gould 1892: 267).

Kissing the bride

The nuptial kiss was a solemn part of the ceremony and was duly directed both by the Sarum and York Uses. Its requirement dates from early Roman times when the first kiss represented a legal bond that sealed all contracts. In some areas the officiating clergyman was also required to kiss the bride which often created awkwardness and embarrassment. Throughout Cleveland, it was the custom for the man who gave away the bride to claim the first kiss in right of his temporary paternity (Henderson 1879: 39). The first person who arrived at the house after the marriage also enjoyed the privilege of kissing the bride. In the border parishes the horses of the attendants were tethered outside the church and as soon as the register was signed, all rushed out of the vestry and a race began, each going across country to win the coveted prize (Vaux 1894: 100).

Post-ceremonial customs and folklore

Brand records that it was customary in most parts of England for the young men present at the service to salute the bride in turn as soon as the ceremony concluded. In pre-modern England it was also the common custom to drink wine in church after the nuptial rites and the Sarum Missal directed that the cup containing it should be blessed by the priest. It was traditional for pieces of cake or wafers, known as 'sops' to be immersed in the wine (Brand 1849: 141, 136-7;). The beverage was drunk not only by the bride and bridegroom but also by the rest of the company. A distinct survival of this custom, although in a modified form, lingered beyond the middle of the nineteenth century at Whitburn, Durham, where it was the custom to give 'hot-pots'. That is, at the conclusion of the marriage service the bride and bridegroom were served in the porch with steaming mixtures of brandy, ale, sugar, eggs and spices. The bridesmaids would also partake in this, and the remainder was distributed amongst the guests (Henderson 1897: 40).

Bad luck and ceremonial subversions

Given the life-changing effects of matrimony, it is not surprising that many superstitious beliefs have come to surround the nuptial rites. Some of these are of a very local nature it and it is difficult to discern their origin. In some areas it was considered unlucky for a bridal procession to pass through a lychgate or enter through the north door of a church (Radford and Radford 1961: 356). Omens portending the death of one or other marriage partner were common. For example, in the north of England, it was thought to be a bad omen for the couple if their marriage took place while there was an open grave in the church yard. In the south of Yorkshire there was a belief that during the marriage ceremony the person who speaks the loudest in answer to the questions put by the clergyman would die first (Vaux 1894: 106). There was also a widespread belief that to drop the wedding ring before or during the marriage service was very unlucky. If it was dropped by the groom or the bride, it was a sign that he or she would die first.

Couples leaving the church after the service would be expected to depart with caution. A Berkshire superstition stated that whichever of the newly married pair stepped out of the church first would be master in the house (Radford and Radford 1949: 253). Bell-ringing immediately after the ceremony is always regarded as a positive element to the proceedings but in some parts of Hertfordshire if the bell-rope happened to break it was considered a bad omen for the couple (Gerish 1911: 5).

Some bizarre customs involving the use of projectile objects against the clergy at marriage services have also been recorded. At Llanedi, Carmarthenshire, in the early nineteenth century, it was customary to bombard the clergyman with quantities of nuts and apples during the wedding service. The incumbent was relaxed about this until a new curate arrived. Upon being hit by nuts he immediately noted the offender, jumped over the altar rails, seized the man and flung him out of a window! The man suffered three broken ribs and predictably, this banished the custom (Baker 1977: 91).

During the eighteenth century at Donington-on-Bain, Lincolnshire it was a custom for elderly women in the parish to assemble in the nave of the church on the occasion of a wedding and, as the bridal party moved up to the chancel, to pelt them with the hassocks. After they had moved beyond the chancel screen, the bride and her attendants were safe, but the old women still continued to hurl the hassocks at each other. Once again it would seem that the incumbent was remarkably tolerant of this strange behaviour in church until a new rector was eventually appointed. During his first wedding in the parish, he was struck by one of the hassocks and his furious response ensured that the custom also came to an abrupt end (Rudkin 1933: 290). A similar custom was recorded up to about 1846 at Barmby Moor, Yorkshire when the unfortunate parson had to dash and take cover in the vestry the moment the service had ended! (Baker 1974: 142). It is possible that these customs had evolved spontaneously as a subversive response to a particular wedding occasion and then became embedded as habitual practice.

Bells and confetti

As soon as the church rites are completed, some form of noise or music is expected as a proclamation and celebration of the marriage. In pre-modern times such noise was also intended to intimidate the malevolent spirit world. It is certainly the custom in all English parishes for the couple to leave the church to the joyful sound of bells. Indeed, at one time in Upton St Leonard, Gloucestershire, people would beat pots and pans to make 'rough music' if the church bells were not rung. In some parts of the country, notably in Yorkshire, the desire for noise extended to the tradition of rifles being fired over the bridal party as they left the church and in some cases, before they arrived for the ceremony (Blakeborough 1898: 101).

In the north of England it was the custom to toll the tenor bell several times as the happy couple left the church to signify how many children they could expect to have! (Camp 1988: 62). There were also customs associated with the bell-ringers and if a member of a ringing team married, the peal was known as a 'wedding compliment'. At Aldington, Worcestershire, even as late as the 1920s, the belfry was decorated with mutton and beef bones which grateful bridegrooms had provided for the ringers (Savory 1920: 94). In Wales, bells seem to have been less popular and as soon as the marriage ceremony was over it was once the custom for a harpist in the churchyard to play an old Welsh air appropriate to the occasion (Davies 1911: 34).

Once out in the churchyard it is still the time-honoured custom to throw paper 'confetti' (Italian, meaning 'sweets') at the bride and groom which emulates the same practice in Italy where sweets are thrown over the couple as they emerge from the church. In some communities raisins, rice, flowers and petals are scattered. Wheat was formerly thrown in Nottinghamshire accompanied with the cheerful shout of 'Bread for life and pudding forever!' In Devon during the nineteenth century, brides were given little bags of hazelnuts as they left the church (Baker 1974: 141, 74). These rituals have no spiritual function but are intended bestow prosperity and fertility on the couple. This is further reinforcement of imitative magic by bringing the couple in contact with seeds and other items connected with biological reproduction to stimulate fecundity.

A popular custom among wedding guests requires the happy couple to walk through arches formed from artefacts representing the trade of the bridegroom. For example, T-squares for draughtsmen, hoes for gardeners and truncheons for policemen. If the groom was a military man, swords would be used (Baker 1977: 105). The arch formed in this way clearly suggests a symbolic entrance to married life. An interesting post-ceremonial custom in a similar vein was upheld at Cranbrook, Kent in the nineteenth century; when a newly married couple left the church, the path was strewn with the emblems of the bridegroom's profession, so carpenters walked on shavings, gardeners on flowers, farmers on cut grass, shoemakers on leather parings, and so on (Vaux 1894: 102–3).

The bride has always been a particular focus of post-ceremonial rituals and, in earlier times, women would try to rip pieces of the bride's dress and flowers in order to obtain some of her good luck. When the bride leaves the church, traditionally to escape from the crowd, she tosses her bouquet into the wedding party and attempts to run away. The bouquet is always eagerly caught by single women in the group in the belief that whoever catches it will be the next to marry. An interesting variation of this custom was practised in the nineteenth century; the principal bridesmaid threw the bride's shoe among the guests and the woman who caught it would be the next to marry; if a man took hold of it he would be the next to wed (Ditchfield 1901: 194).

Lifting the bride

A common custom in northern England was to challenge the newlyweds to jump or be lifted over some obstacle in the churchyard immediately after the service. The most noteworthy example of this tradition is the ritual conducted over the 'Petting Stone' at Whittingham parish church, Northumberland. Two young men who were generally close friends of the bride and bridegroom were told to 'jump' the bride over the stone. The bridegroom and the remainder of the wedding party were then vaulted over in the same manner. If the vicar was in a happy disposition he was reported to have also joined in the fun. It was said that the bride must leave all her 'pets' or sullen moods behind her when she crosses it and if she refused, she was said to have 'taken the pet' and this would meet with general disapproval (Crooke 1902: 226-251). A refusal was also considered to indicate that the marriage would prove to be unfortunate.

A similar stone formerly known as the 'socket stone' still exists in the grounds adjoining Lindisfarne Abbey on Holy Island and there is an example at Durham Cathedral. A number of other villages, such as Belford and Bamburgh performed improvised versions of this practice. At Embleton, for example, young men placed a wooden bench across the door of the church porch and followed the same procedure. A donation from the bridegroom was expected and the men would often scramble for money that had been scattered around the church (Henderson 1897: 38).

In Cleveland, the bride and groom would similarly leap over a bench and afterwards a gun charged with feathers was fired. It has been suggested that this 'symbolised a wish that nothing harder might ever fall upon them' (Nicholson 1890: 3). These group rituals have been interpreted as fertility charms, although those connected to the threshold may have been intended as protection against evil influences which may beset the couple at the beginning of their married life (Crooke 1902: 251).

Barring the way

A wedding couple departing from the church could also find themselves being challenged by some form of barricade, which required a toll to be paid before they could pass through. Typically, the churchyard gates would be tied or a rope or pole placed across their path. There are many variants of 'barring the way' and it is still widespread in many European countries. In Somerset, for example, the village children used to fasten the gates of the church with evergreens and flowers, until money was given to allow them to leave (*Notes and Queries* [1858] 5: 178–9). Similarly at Crosby Ravensworth, Westmoreland, children from the village school gathered around the church door and held the handle to prevent the exit of the wedding party until the bridegroom passed a coin under the door. A further boisterous scramble for a halfpenny was also undertaken at the churchyard gate (Vaux 1894: 105). In most versions of the custom it is the bridegroom who pays the toll and as marriages traditionally took place in the bride's parish, it was seen as a means for the husband to symbolically pay his way into the community (Monger 2004: 20). However, the marriage as a rite of passage also appears to be confirmed in this ritual.

As soon as the married couple had been allowed to leave the churchyard the wedding party would then proceed home for the 'wedding breakfast', rich with its own traditions to conclude the celebrations of the day. The final part of the nuptial contract was the consummation of the marriage and prior to the seventeenth century in England it was not unusual for the church to provide a 'wedding house' where the continuing revelry could take place. This building would often contain a bedchamber with a bridal bed, such as the example at Braughing in Hertfordshire (Monger 2004: 23). At the end of the day the bedding of the couple was initiated with considerable ceremonial, but this only began after the parish priest had first blessed the bed.

Chapter Nine

Death:

Funeral Customs and Beliefs

Death is the final great transition and change. Death has never been considered a purely natural event and in former times it was always attended with magical influences and superstitious practices. Popular religion came to the fore to assist in managing the care and disposal of the dead and the rituals surrounding death continue to address deep spiritual and emotional needs. In this chapter, we will explore the customs and traditions that have supported funeral rites in both official and popular Christianity.

Watching for death

In the modern world, discussion about death is something that most people try to avoid but in the Middle Ages, when life was more fragile and uncertain, death was more of a preoccupation than it is now. Death seemed to be predicted in countless human actions and natural phenomena. It could be announced through a variety of portents and signs such as howling dogs, a cock crowing, loud knocks, a broken glass, a picture falling or tapping at windows by robins or magpies. Even in church, the clock striking, bells ringing and other spontaneous happenings at unusual or unfortunate moments in a service could signal imminent death. These portents were taken seriously well into the nineteenth century and although they had no objective truth, they 'acted as a *memento mori* in an age and society in which death came suddenly, unpredictably and early in life' (Obelkevich 1976: 295).

The fascination with impending mortality was the focus of a strange custom known as 'porch-watching' which took place on St Mark's Eve (24 April). This was traditionally a popular evening for marriage divination rituals but the ghoulish purpose of this particular observance was to discover who in the parish was going to die within the next twelve months. Anyone wishing to find out this information would go to the church porch at a late hour on 24 April and wait there until midnight. At about this time it was believed that a spectral funeral procession of all those expected to die during the coming year could be seen passing into the church (Wright and Lones 1938 Vol 2: 189–91).

Porch-watching had many variations and was particularly common in Yorkshire parishes where these vigils usually had to be undertaken for an hour either side of midnight over three successive years. In some parishes it was not unknown for the observers to obtain a considerable income from divulging their findings to those wishing to know their fate in the year ahead (Nicholson 1890: 84–5). The custom is also widely recorded in other northern counties up to the mid-nineteenth century. There was a similar observance in Wales where, even into the twentieth century, it was thought that one could see who was going to die in the parish in the forthcoming year by looking into the keyhole of the church at midnight on Halloween (Owen 1991: 38).

The passing bell

When a parishioner was dying the first alert to the community would have been the ringing of the 'passing bell' to invite others to pray for the safe passing of his soul. This is an early medieval custom, originally intended to drive away an evil spirit who might be waiting to seize the soul of the deceased. It was sometimes known as the 'soul bell' because its spiritual intention was to signify the 'passing' of the soul out of this life (Vaux 1894: 123). Occasionally the 'death knell' was tolled immediately after a death but still retained the incorrect name of the passing bell. However, a very practical function of this bell was to summon the priest to comfort the sick person and to administer the last rites. The use of the passing bell was another custom that came under attack from the Puritans although it lingered on into the early twentieth century in some rural parishes.

For a typical family in pre-modern England, the most immediate requirement was to ensure that all doors and windows of the house were opened to ease the departure of the soul. Fires were sometimes put out and the clocks stopped, and these actions were probably intended to mark the transition from time to eternity (Simpson and Roud 2004: 93). More recently it was a convention throughout the country to close curtains upon the death of the occupant. As soon as death had occurred, the corpse was considered to be extremely vulnerable and a prey to evil spirits, so ritual 'wakes' or vigils were held although these also had a very practical function. In the days when medical science was undeveloped, sitting and praying with the body allowed mourners to check if the person watched was really dead or only in an unconscious state. After the beginning of the seventeenth century these wakes developed into occasions where food, drink and lights would be provided. Sometimes these gatherings could develop into ribald parties, but this behaviour probably helped 'ease the tension aroused by death and countered the threat of annihilation with jokes about procreation' (Jupp and Gittings 1999: 153).

Preparing the corpse

Before the mid-nineteenth century, the responsibility for preparing the corpse and organising the practical elements of the funeral rested with the family. The body would be 'laid out' and washed in a ritual fashion by the women of the family or done by hired women who were often local midwives. Afterwards the corpse would be placed in a shroud or stitched into a winding-sheet. Sometimes, sprigs of rosemary, yew, box or rue were put into the shroud and flowers might also be displayed around the corpse in wealthier households. By mid-Victorian times the middle classes had placed these arrangements in the hands of professional undertakers, but working-class funerals were still basically family affairs until the twentieth century. In early medieval times if a corpse had to be conveyed over some distance it was wrapped in ox hide. Linen was more commonly used and only the prosperous were permitted to be 'chested' or placed in a coffin. The poor were generally buried in canvas although in 1666 an Act of Parliament was passed insisting that all people should be buried in a shroud made of wool rather than linen. This developed from an increasing concern over the wasteful use of cotton materials but the law was often flouted (Puckle 1926, 2008: 23). During the time the Act was in force corpses were sometimes covered simply with hay or flowers (Vaux 1894: 145). Interestingly, in the Book of Common Prayer the word coffin is not even mentioned, but burial is anticipated with the words: 'the earth shall be cast upon the body'.

Coffins started to become popular for burials in the mid-seventeenth century. By concealing bodily decay in this way it increased the social distancing of the living from the dead. Coffins were generally made of oak or elm and sometimes richly lined, which meant they could be expensive and therefore effective status symbols among the wealthy classes (Puckle 1926, 2008: 29). If poorer families wished to use a coffin, the only dignified option was the temporary use of a 'parish coffin' which was usually kept at the church and

*Parish Coffin at church of
St Peter, Howden, Yorkshire.*

intended only for conveying the body to the graveside. After the body had been placed in the grave it was covered by a shroud or a winding-sheet and the coffin was returned for re-use. In medieval times, each parish had a burial guild, which eased the financial burden on the poor by supplying bearers to carry the corpse and the parish coffin. Some paupers were buried in very basic coffins of cheap timber which were pushed on a hand cart and may have been covered with a pall. Clearly some churches wished to make it plain that they made charitable provisions for the dead. St John's Westminster for example, ordered that only a cloth pall should be used, and that it should bear upon it the words, 'buried at the expense of the parish' (Vaux 1894: 146).

Burial with grave goods

The archaic practice of placing coins, jewellery and even food and drink with the deceased to ease the journey into the afterlife has been remarkably persistent even into recent times. In pagan burials and cremations it was usual for the body to be accompanied by possessions used in life. The early Church abolished this custom for ordinary people although priests, monks and nuns were permitted to be placed in their coffins dressed in their religious vestments and habits. In medieval times it was customary to present a priest at his ordination with a chalice and, at death this was also put into the grave with him and placed upright at the side of the body (Gilchrist 1967: 18–19). Bishops and abbots nearly always had their rings and crosiers buried with them. It gradually became customary for the laity to be buried in attire of their choosing and in the Middle Ages it was considered most honourable for a knight to be buried in full armour (Andrews 1895: 132). The custom of dressing the deceased in special clothes is still common and the chosen attire may reflect their vocation or passionate communal concerns and interests. Burial clothes might typically include wedding dresses, old military uniforms, team uniforms, sports clothes, favourite casual garments or suits.

While a corpse was being prepared for burial it was an old practice to place coins in the mouth 'to give to St Peter' (Wilson 2004: 297). Coins would be laid on the eyes for the same purpose, although these also had the practical purpose of keeping eyelids closed until they stiffened. Significant quantities of silver and copper coins have been found in English churchyards, which reinforces the perception that the necessity of money in temporal life was also believed to be a requirement for the afterlife (Puckle 1926, 2008: 32). In addition to money and jewellery, many types of articles have been placed in the coffin, including photos of loved ones, a Bible, musical instrument, official regalia, walking sticks or any other object that was of great personal significance to the deceased. A common but locally variable practice was to place flowers in the coffin. So for example, in Monmouthshire, plants such as hyssop or wormwood were placed with the corpse as a symbol of repentance (Wherry 1905: 66), while in Shropshire it was the custom to put roses and wallflowers inside the coffin (Burne 1883: 299). Possibly these were intended as love tokens.

The ancient custom of sacrificing animals and placing them with the deceased still lingered even up to the early twentieth century. Among the working classes of London there were reports of pets being killed and placed with their owners in the coffin, or buried in the garden of the deceased as companions into the afterlife (Lovett 1925: 35, 48). Sometimes articles placed with the corpse were intended to have a specific post-mortem function. In Wiltshire, for example, when a shepherd died there was a touching custom of placing a piece of wool in his coffin with the notion that on the Day of Judgement he could prove his lonely vocation, which would sometimes have prevented him from attending regularly at church (Law 1900: 345). It is still quite common for objects and flowers to be dropped onto the coffin during the committal and for articles, including food or drink to be left on the grave soon after the funeral.

The funeral procession

After preparations had been prepared, friends and other members of the community were invited or 'bidden' to the funeral. In Westmoreland, very large numbers of friends and neighbours were invited by messengers sent on 'bidding rounds'. One or two persons were invited from each family and were bidden to be at the house of the deceased for about 10 a.m.. In the north of England this was known as the hour of 'lifting the corpse' and the term also described the entertainment provided for visitors. In Wales, following a tradition found worldwide, professional 'wailers' were sometimes employed; these were women who could maintain an outpouring of emotion with wild demonstrations of grief in return for a modest fee (Puckle 1926, 2008: 45). It was customary to provide some refreshment for mourners before the funeral, which may have taken place at home or more usually in a village inn.

Rural funerals among the poor were usually simple occasions and mourners processed to the church on foot. By contrast, the funerals of the wealthy and the nobility were lavish affairs involving long processions of mourners, initially on foot but later by carriage. Eventually the deceased were transported in increasingly elaborate horse-drawn hearses with displays of black plumes and velvet drapes. The proceedings would be supported by silent professional mourners known as 'mutes', dressed in black and wearing melancholy expressions appropriate to the occasion. However, some funerals were not silent affairs and hymn singing was common in rural processions (Vaux 1894: 130).

In a simple 'walking funeral', the bearers were good friends and relatives, and where possible, they were chosen to reflect the status of the deceased. Older members of the community, especially if they were married, would be carried by married men; unmarried girls were carried by young women, although if the road was long and arduous, young bachelors might be asked to take on the role. In Cornwall it was an old custom at children's funerals for young girls, dressed in light colours, to carry one of their own sex and age to the grave. The usual method of carrying was to rest the coffin on shoulders, although in some parts of the country, napkins or towels were passed underneath it and wrapped around the forearms of the bearers (Vaux 1894: 126, 127). In areas where the parish church was at a considerable distance, the body was carried on a portable bier and there were 'resting stones' set at intervals along the roadside on which to place it while the bearers changed sides. Carrying a coffin could be physically demanding work and mourners who assembled to escort the body were customarily fortified with beer, wine or spirits (Cressy 1997: 444). In some localities it was the custom to distribute a sweet, fruity cake known as 'arval bread' to the mourners before starting the procession.

Funeral attire

Dress codes at funerals have always been very specific and black attire has traditionally signified mourning in Britain. However, medieval sumptuary laws established clear rules for dress, and the practice of wearing black during a time of bereavement was not followed by the lower classes until much later. Inevitably, local dress customs began to evolve. For example, at Arundel, Sussex, black and white 'frocks' were worn by the poorer male parishioners (Vaux 1894: 125–6). Mourners of higher social status generally wore long trains and hoods made of expensive, dull black wool trimmed with black or white crepe or linen. Widows, in particular, wore mourning dress, called 'widow's weeds', complete with a veil if they were expected to be outside for a period of time. The coffin bearers rarely had their own specific dress code although in Lincolnshire, until the mid-nineteenth century the interment of a woman who had died in childbirth was known as a 'white funeral', and the corpse was carried by women wearing white hoods (Gutch and Peacock 1908: 236). The priest wore surplice, cassock and black stole, although in Staffordshire, Derbyshire, and the West Riding of Yorkshire it was also customary for the cleric to wear a broad black silk scarf with a shoulder knot, provided by the friends of the deceased (Vaux 1894: 125–6). The parish clerk was usually dressed like the poorer members of the congregation, in a white or slate coloured frock. Graveside funerals conducted in the rain are always particularly miserable occasions and it is a curious fact that before the umbrella came into general use in Britain it was first employed by the clergy at funerals as a means of protection against wet weather! (Andrews 1900: 224).

Corpse roads

In many remote country areas, the roads could be poor and the final journey from the home of the deceased to the local church could be fraught with difficulties. A more direct route could sometimes be found across neighbouring farmland and there was once a widespread belief that if a corpse was carried over fields on the way to burial, it established a permanent right of way. Carrying a corpse over private ground from a remote dwelling would have been a frequent occurrence and undertakers would stick a number of pins into each gate as the procession walked to the church. This action indicated that a right of way had been granted only for this particular occasion and was accepted by the landowner as payment for the privilege (Andrews 1895: 140) although such arrangements had no actual foundation in English law.

The belief that they created a permanent right of public access is perpetuated by their descriptions such as 'corpse-ways', 'lych-ways' or 'church-roads'. Local superstition developed to ensure that the person to be buried was only carried by this established route as it was believed that he or she would not rest quietly in their grave if taken to the church by any other route (Atkinson 1868: 593). Straight routes were usually favoured and this may be connected to the universal belief that spirits of the dead fly close to the ground and always in a straight line. The presence of corpse-ways can still be discerned in the names of certain country roads. There is a 'Burial Road' at Feckenham, Worcestershire and near Burry Port in Camarthenshire there is a bridleway that is known locally as the 'Coffin Trail'.

Arriving at the churchyard

The funeral party would arrive at the churchyard to be met by the priest, and lych-gates (see Chapter 3) provided temporary shelter for the bearers and the coffin if the weather was wet. There was often great concern over the prospect of a wedding and a funeral party meeting at the church gate at the same time which was believed to bring misfortune. Great efforts would be made to ensure this did not happen and at Madeley, Shropshire two gates were provided; it was customary for the weddings to use the right-hand entrance and funerals to enter by the left-hand gate. Both parties would enter by the same church door but the provision of two gates helped to minimise the risk of meeting (Dyer 1891: 156–7).

There was also a belief in Yorkshire and other parts of the country that a funeral procession must necessarily go to the churchyard by the way which will make the party meet the sun in its course. This was known as 'the way of the sun', or 'going the back way' and some people would go to any length at funerals to ensure that they followed the sun (Henderson 1879: 61). The direction in which the body was carried through the church precincts was also important. Suffolk churches have a north and south door and the body was usually carried through the south door, put down at the west end of the aisle, and subsequently taken out by the north door. In Lincolnshire, the north door was used only for funerals, with the south and west doors reserved for christenings and weddings (Andrews 1895: 137).

Funeral bells

Parish bells also had their own codes at funerals. After the passing bell came the 'death knell' which announced a death had occurred. A number of different peals were used to indicate age and gender of the deceased: nine strokes for a man; six for a woman; three for a child. These strokes were called 'tellers' and probably gave rise to a former saying 'nine tailors (tellers) made a man' (Vaux 1894: 124). In medieval times, the ringing of bells was also believed to help the passage of the deceased by driving away evil spirits and sometimes peals would continue for many hours or even days. The sound of bells at funerals was also considered to be a spiritual benefit for the living, because it encouraged them to pray for the deceased and meditate on their own mortality.

Many local ringing customs prevailed and in some Buckinghamshire parishes for example, a bell was tolled about an hour before the beginning of a funeral to summon the bearers (Cocks 1894: 278). Small hand-held 'dead bells' were commonly used in pre-Reformation times to clear a passage for a funeral procession and to call for prayers for the deceased (Andrews, 1899: 36). In parts of Wales during the nineteenth century a 'corpse bell' or 'lyche bell' was rung by a bellman, who would usually be the parish clerk, walking just ahead of the procession (Owen 1987: 176–7). Bell-ringing at funerals was moderated in the Elizabethan period and Puritan activists were always keen to diminish their superstitious associations.

Flowers at funerals

Plants and flowers have always had an important role in funeral rites and strewing flowers on coffins and graves was a widespread practice. Although strongly scented evergreen plants were used to mask the odour of putrefaction while the dead were laid out at home before burial, they also contained strong significations of immortality (Drury 1994: 101). There were many regional variations of this practice and at Filey, Yorkshire, for instance, rosemary, ivy and laurel was taken to the graveside (Cole 1828: 138) while in Derbyshire, sprigs of box and yew were carried and subsequently dropped on to the coffin (*Notes and Queries* [1914] 9: 297). Yew was popular as a resurrection symbol because of its ability to regenerate from an apparently dead root; this has been offered as an explanation for its frequent occurrence as a churchyard tree. Rosemary was favoured at funerals as the herb of remembrance. It was considered a serious breach of decorum for any mourner to appear at a funeral without a sprig of rosemary which would be thrown into the grave after the coffin had been lowered.

Certain death situations had their own specific flower codes. So for example, lovers who had the misfortune to die before their wedding day had garlands of willow, yew and rosemary laid on their biers (Drury 1994: 103). The more conventional practice of placing a wreath on the coffin is a fairly recent custom, and was established towards the end of the nineteenth century, encouraged by the example of Queen Victoria and the royal family (Vickery 1995: 144–5).

The choice of flowers was often directed by the appropriateness of their colour for mourning. The common mallow was often used to decorate graves, because its dark green foliage and purple flowers were suggestive of mourning. The colour could also say something about the status of the deceased and red roses spoke of a life of goodness while white signified a virgin (Drury 1994: 102). Sometimes the symbolism could take a more sinister turn and plants such as nettles and thistles might be mischievously placed or planted on the graves of those who had been disliked in life.

Burial locations and customs of grave construction

In pre-modern England the choice of burial location within the church precincts was often a matter of great concern and there was always a preference for burial near the church building. In this way, the dead were physically in close proximity to the liturgy and the mass and in some parishes, possibly the relics of the saints (Wilson 2004: 297). The south side was popular, maybe because the churchyard cross was located there but also because it received the sun. The south door was the principal entrance and highly prized for burials because tombs would be in sight of relatives and friends (*Notes and Queries* [1850] 2: 189).

Indoor burial was popular possibly because it was warmer and more sheltered, but also because up to the seventeenth century the irrational idea prevailed that the dead were in some sense still responsive to their surroundings (Tarlow 2011: 173). Interment in a church wall was greatly favoured because it was believed to give some kind of immunity from the claims of both God and the Devil (Baker-Jones, 1977: 81). Wall burials were common and sometimes in an erect posture, which was particularly fashionable among army captains who died in battle. There are instances of vertical pillar burials at churches in Narburgh and Clarborough, Nottinghamshire (Dyer 1891: 142, 144, 135) and there is an example under a pillar at York Minster. At the end of the seventeenth century, Job Orton, an innkeeper, was buried on his own instructions in an erect posture, in the hope that he would rise before his wife, who was interred in the usual fashion (*Notes and Queries* [1853] 8: 59). The poet and actor Ben Jonson, was also buried in this manner at Westminster Abbey, ostensibly to avoid the large fee demanded for a full-sized grave (Vaux 1894: 151).

The cost of a church burial could vary considerably depending on location and the payment was often known as 'pit money', which churchwardens considered to be a lucrative boost to church funds. Often the custom was taken to excess and churches became packed with corpses in shallow graves which were constantly being disturbed by new arrivals. This unhygienic situation has been cited as one of the primary causes of the constant outbreaks of plague in the sixteenth and seventeenth centuries (Cox 1913: 169). Despite this concern, church interments continued until the late eighteenth century and special requests were occasionally made for a particular location. An intriguing example is the grave of Nicholas Broome at Baddesley Clinton in Warwickshire, who is assumed to be buried under the floor of the church, because he requested in his will 'that my body may be buried in the parish church... where as many people may tread upon me when they come into church'. This was believed to be part of his penance for two murders he had committed (Palmer 1976: 36).

Graves within the churchyard are usually of simple construction but there have been a variety of distinctive local customs prior to burial. During the early medieval period they could be lined with mortar, stone or tile as at the church of St Nicholas Shambles, London (Carver 1987: 95). Graves lined with charcoal have been discovered at locations as diverse as Worcester, Exeter, Winchester, Oxford and York and many of the bodily remains have accompanied by 'pillow stones' either side of the head to keep it in position. These graves may represent the burials of churchmen and women of high rank and these arrangements might possibly be an intuitive response to the belief that disease and death is a punishment for sin and that a well-preserved body has a better chance of salvation (Jupp and Gittings 1999: 86). By contrast, brick-lined graves became increasingly common during the eighteenth and nineteenth centuries, primarily because of the fear of being buried alive.

Burial of the unbaptised

Babies who died without baptism did not fare well when it came to a burial and hard-line clergy are recorded as refusing to bury them even as late as the nineteenth century (Cressy 1997: 117). The north side of the churchyard was known as the 'wrong side of the church' and there babies, together with suicides, the insane and criminals were buried although frequently such people were interred outside sacred ground. Suicide was regarded as a profound mortal sin and the best that a self-murderer could expect was burial by a crossroads, with its tenuous reference to the Christian cross (Crooke 1909: 88–9). As a final protective measure, bodies buried in unhallowed ground had a stake driven through them to hold them down and prevent the corpse walking as a ghost.

The dead who were placed in unconsecrated ground were placed beyond the symbolic community of the dead and outside the protection afforded by the Church. This controversial situation remained until 1823, when an Act of Parliament was passed ordering parishes to allocate a piece of unconsecrated ground for those traditionally denied a Christian burial. In East Anglia, such deceased persons were said to 'lie out of the sanctuary' (Forby 1830: 407). Prostitutes usually received an equally humble burial, and in Southwark in London, there was formerly an unconsecrated burial ground called the 'Single Woman's Churchyard' in which were interred the inmates of the licensed brothels or 'stews', who were generally excommunicated (Burns 1862: 107).

Funeral rite and graveside committal

Traditionally, the body of the deceased remained at home until the day of the interment, but it is also an ancient custom for the coffin to be received into the church the night before the burial. Nowadays in many Anglican churches the coffin is met by the priest at the church door and it may be sprinkled with holy water on arrival. In a traditional funeral, the coffin is led into the church and placed in front of the altar, where a short rite known as the 'Office of the Dead', comprising psalms, readings and prayers, is celebrated by all present. The bier is surrounded by candles reflecting the spiritual meaning of the opening words of the Requiem Mass which follows: 'Rest eternal grant them,

Lord, and light perpetual shine upon them'. The importance of light was emphasised in the tradition followed in some churches, of breaking up the Paschal candle after Trinity Sunday every year to provide a supply of lights for the funerals of the poor (Rock 1853: 379). During the mass, the body was censed and a short homily or sermon would ensue. In sixteenth and seventeenth century high society, funeral sermons were considered almost mandatory (Dyer 1891: 138), after which gifts of wine, wafers, gloves, ribbons and rosemary were distributed to those who attended. A Mass is now far less common at an Anglican funeral and the rite is a much simpler form, commending the soul of the deceased to God's keeping.

After the service the coffin is taken to the graveside, or to a crematorium. The corpse is always carried feet first in a funeral procession and placing the body in the grave with the correct orientation has always been considered important. Burying the dead with feet towards the east was the usual custom in England and the body was 'buried face up to meet the angel of the resurrection' (Cressy 1997: 466). A clergyman was usually buried facing west, so that he could rise facing his flock. These sensibilities were taken very seriously and even bodies laid in the plague pits of London at the time of the Black Death were placed with a care for the correct orientation (Hawkins 1990: 637–42). In parts of South Wales, an east wind was often aptly described as the 'wind from the feet of the dead', a phrase that was still current into the mid-twentieth century (Lloyd 1945: 307).

As soon as the coffin is lowered into the grave there is a key point in the committal where the words beginning 'Earth to earth, ashes to ashes... .' are recited, while a handful of earth is symbolically cast onto the coffin by the priest. At this point offerings are made and some mourners may throw gloves, flowers or other items into the grave. Floral tributes from mourners are placed on the grave. In some parts of the country after the rite has concluded it is traditional for close relatives to remain until the grave has been filled.

Maidens' garlands

In many parts of the country there was a special funeral custom for unmarried girls. Garlands or 'virgins' crowns', adorned with flowers and paper trimmings were carried by maidens like bridesmaids at the funeral of a spinster. The garland was then hung in the church after the funeral. The crown was only awarded if the deceased had been born, baptised, died unmarried in the parish and was of exceptionally good character. The practice of hanging garlands can be traced back to the sixteenth century but is considered to derive from the early days of Christianity when funeral garlands were emblems of virgin martyrs. Records exist from many parishes, with notable examples at Chester in Kent, Walsingham in Norfolk, Stanhope

Maidens garlands in St Stephen's church, Fylingdales, North Yorkshire. Photograph by Doc Rowe.

in Co. Durham, at Bolton-in-Craven and Skipton in Yorkshire. The custom continued until recent times and the most recent funeral of this kind took place at St Mary's, Abbotts Ann, Hampshire in 1973.

The garlands were solemnly carried before the coffin during the funeral procession by two young girls, dressed in white and during the church service the crown was suspended from a white rod or placed upon the coffin (Andrews 1890: 148). Typically, the mourners were dressed in white not in black (Wilson 2004: 305). After the funeral the crown was suspended from the front gallery for three weeks and, if it was not challenged, it was then hung from a bracket near the ceiling of the church with a shield bearing the name and date (King 1992). Another custom at the interment of a spinster, known in Leicestershire, but also apparently occurring elsewhere, was that of welcoming the corpse to the church with a merry peal of bells accompanied by the giving of some form of gift to neighbours and friends of the deceased (North 1876: 110).

Nocturnal burials

Burials at night by torchlight were especially popular during the eighteenth century. These funerals were common among royalty and certain aristocratic families (Dyer 1891: 138) and in some cases were undertaken for the sake of secrecy or perhaps where the deceased was a controversial figure. The word funeral, properly refers to a torchlight and is derived from the Latin, *funeralis*, which itself originates from *funis*, a torch. Even when the practice of nocturnal burial was discontinued, torches were still carried at funeral processions and placed about the body until time of burial. George II was buried in this manner in Westminster Abbey in 1760. Up to the seventeenth century, Aldermen of the City of London, who had served their mayoralty, were by ancient custom 'buried with speedy solemnity and usually by torchlight but these occasions invariably degenerated into scenes of disorder and were banned by Charles I (Dyer 1891: 140).

It has been suggested that night burials could have had an original function to scare away evil spirits (Puckle 1926, 2008: 51), but their later popularity was probably explained by the greater emphasis they gave to feelings of sorrow and loss; the darkness and torchlight fostered the atmosphere of gloom and reflected the emotions of grief at bereavement (Jupp and Gittings 1999: 162). The torches were made from pieces of rope dipped in tar and were often provided by the churchwardens; parish accounts suggest that the Church made a small profit from these. Many people would make provision in their wills for candles or the burning of torches at their funerals, and these were often large in size and supplied great in number (Dendy 1959: 101–2).

In the early nineteenth century there was a curious nocturnal burial custom at Skipton in West Yorkshire whereby a woman who had died at the birth of her first child was buried at midnight; the coffin was carried under a white sheet, the corners of which were held by four women (Andrews 1895: 142). There is a strong parallel here with the 'white funerals' custom mentioned above, where a woman who had died in this way had a white pall placed over her coffin (Brand 1949 Vol 2: 284; Gutch and Peacock 1908: 236).

A footnote on cremation

In more recent times, cremation has become the most popular method of disposing of the dead. Although the practice of cremation dates from pre-history, it was unacceptable to early Christians because it appeared to compromise belief in the resurrection and so generally lost support among the faithful throughout the Roman Empire. Pressure on cemetery space and issues of sanitation encouraged a reappraisal of cremation amongst the freethinkers of the nineteenth century. The first official cremation in Britain took place in 1885 at Woking and since the 1930s it has become the preferred form of disposal for about seventy percent of deaths in Great Britain. For many Christians it begins with a service in their own church, followed by a committal in the crematorium chapel, but for many funerals of all faiths and none, the crematorium alone is the chosen location for the funeral rites.

Venetia Newall has made an exhaustive study of the folklore that has developed around the culture of cremation (Newall 1985). However, many of the folk beliefs that are reported are not necessarily those of the Christian community, given that secular and humanist funerals are common in crematoria. An urban legend before the Second World War maintained that cancer was unclean and contagious. If a cancer victim was buried, the cancer was believed to infect the ground and cremation seemed a more hygienic way forward, because it would destroy the germs (Newall 1985: 141).

Most of the folklore that has evolved generally focuses on the cremation process itself. For example, there is a common belief that coffins are recycled or that several bodies are cremated together. The natural horror of fire also underpins many beliefs and many people are convinced that when the coffin disappears from view, it enters directly into the incinerator; others have reported that they can see flames beyond the curtains.

There is of course no substance to any of these beliefs and as Newall points out, many of the common misconceptions have developed from 'ignorance of the cremation process and the general air of mystery surrounding what goes on out of sight (Newall 1985: 143). The continuing unease about the use of cremation expressed by many individuals may also stem from the modern perception of death as an unnatural obscenity and a fear of loss of personality when a body is committed to the flames. For Christians and others who believe in post-mortem survival, there may be the subconscious fear that the soul may not survive the process of incineration; there is also the association of fire in a spiritual sense with Hell, sin and the Devil as well as human physical discomfort (Newall 1985: 151). Clearly, in spite of its popularity, there remains a lingering suspicion among many believers and non-believers alike, that cremation is a mysterious, unnatural and alien import to Western culture.

After the funeral

In contemporary life, the payment of funeral fees takes place discreetly before or after the funeral, but in pre-modern times it was usually to settle this debt on the day with the parish clerk. Clerks could do particularly well in Wales for the parish registers of Tregaron, Cardiganshire states that at the death of every married man, he was entitled to the best hat, clothes and shoes of the deceased and, for every woman, he could lay claim to her hat, best shoes and stockings (Dyer 1891: 150). Gravediggers also had to be paid and in the early nineteenth century it was the custom in some parishes in Wales for the sexton to collect the offerings on his spade at the grave side (Aubrey 1881: 219; Vaux 1894: 139–40). Gratuities could also given in the form of food and drink as at Amersden, Oxfordshire, where it was an old custom for a cake and flagon of ale to be given to the minister in the church porch immediately after the funeral (Andrews 1895: 135–6). However, a charitable spirit often prevailed and burial offerings were not always retained for the benefit of the clergyman or church officials; in some places they would go to the family of the deceased, especially if they were of limited means. Only in comparatively recent times when professional undertakers became involved in arrangements were fixed scales of fees applied.

The funeral breakfast

After the interment, it has always been traditional for a 'funeral feast' or 'wake' to take place. The funeral feast in early modern England was sometimes held in the churchyard or within the church itself, but more usually in the family home. Prior to the Reformation it was a common practice for wealthy testators to direct in their wills that doles of money, bread, beer and other alms should be given to the poor at their funerals. These events could attract large crowds and so they performed a double act relieving the corporal wants of the poor and securing their prayers for the repose of their own souls. In modern times the wake often takes the form of a buffet meal, although now more often held in a hotel or pub than at home.

The responsibility of the Church to the deceased family concluded after the funeral rites although it is now popular to hold a memorial service at a specified interval after the interment, to celebrate public aspects of the career and achievements of the deceased.

Gazetteer of church customs through the calendar year

The date and status of the events below were correct at the time of going to press. It is advisable to check dates, times and venues before visiting.

December/January

Christmas Season — Christingle Services
Various churches.

January

early January — Pilgrimages to see the Blossoming of the Holy Thorn
St John's Church, Glastonbury, Somerset

first Monday in January — Landletting of the Poor's Pasture
The George, Hubberholme, North Yorkshire.

6 January — Offering Epiphany gifts to the Monarch
Chapel Royal, St James' Palace, London

Epiphany Carol Services and Processions
Cathedrals at Salisbury, Manchester and Chichester

Greek Orthodox Sea Blessing
Margate and Hastings, Kent.

6 January or Sunday after — Blessing of the River Thames
London Bridge

Sunday after 6 January — Blessing of the Plough
Exeter and Chichester Cathedrals;
Curry Mallet, Somerset

first Monday after 6 January — Plough Monday Procession and Plough Blessing
St Andrew's Church, Northwold, Norfolk

Thursday after Plough Monday	Jankyn Smith Charity St Mary's Church, Bury St Edmunds, Suffolk
30 January	Charles I Wreath-laying and Memorial Service Banqueting House, Whitehall, London
Late January	Katherine of Aragon Festival and Memorial Services Peterborough Cathedral

February

first Sunday in February	Clowns' Service Holy Trinity Church, Dalston, East London
2 February (Candlemas)	Candlemas Services and Blessing of Candles Various churches
	Cradle-Rocking ceremony Blidworth, Notts
	Candlelit Procession Ripon Cathedral
3 February	St Blaise Blessing of water St Mary's Abbey, Bergholt, Suffolk
	The Blessing of Throats St Ethelreda's, (Roman Catholic) London
20 February	Sir John Cass Red Feather Day St Botolph-without-Aldgate, London

February/March

Shrove Tuesday	Ringing the 'Shriving bell' Burgh-le-Marsh, Lincolnshire
	Pancake Race and Shriving Service St Peter and St Paul, Olney, Buckinghamshire
Ash Wednesday	Imposition of Ashes Various churches

March

a date in March	Oranges and Lemons Service St Clement Danes, Strand, London
1 March	St David's Day processions and services Various parishes in England and Wales

10 March (or near date)	The Handy Sermon St Giles' Oxford
fourth Sunday in Lent	Mothering Sunday service and distribution of flowers, etc. Various churches
	Clypping the Church St Lawrence, Upwey, Somerset
Palm Sunday	Processions and distribution of palms Various churches
	Distribution of Pax Cakes St Tysillios, Sellack; St John the Baptist Kings, Caple, Herefordshire
	Battle of Towton Commemoration Service Towton, Yorkshire
Eastertide	Bread and Cheese Dole Biddenden, Kent
Maundy Thursday	Foot-washing Ceremony and Stripping of the Altar Various churches
	Royal Maundy Distribution A UK cathedral (location varies every year)
	Henry Travice Memorial Leigh, Greater Manchester
Good Friday	Stations of the Cross service Various churches
	The Three Hours Service Various churches
	Walk of Witness Various churches
	Hot Cross Buns Distribution St Bartholomew-the-Great, Smithfield, London
	The Hartfield Dole St Mary the Virgin, Hartfield, East Sussex
Easter Saturday	Blessing of New Fire; Procession of Light; Lighting of Paschal Candle Various churches

	Singing over William Hubbards Grave St Mary-in-Arden church, Market Harborough, Leicestershire
Easter Day	Dawn open-air services Various churches
	Eucharist and Easter Egg distributions Various churches
Easter Monday	Clypping the Church St Mary the Virgin, Wirksworth, Derbyshire; St Lawrence, Upwey, Dorset
	Hare-pie Scramble and Bottle-kicking Hallaton, Leicestershire
first or second Sunday after Easter	Family service Taylor Charity and Bun Service St Leonard's Church, Keevil, Wiltshire
second Wednesday after Easter	The Spital Sermon St Lawrence Jewry, City of London

April

A date in April	Harness Horse Blessing Picton Castle, Pembrokeshire
5 April or near date every three years	Changing John Stow's Quill St Andrew's Undershaft, City of London
second Wednesday after Easter	The Spital Sermon St Lawrence Jewry Church, City of London
23 April	Service for the Order of St Michael & St George St Paul's Cathedral, City of London
	St George Memorial Service St George's Chapel, Windsor
	St George's Day Bell-ringing Various churches
Sunday nearest 23 April	Scout Parades and Services Various locations

May

1 May	Singing the Hymnus Eucharisticus The top of Magdalen Tower, Oxford
	Garland Ceremony St Mary the Virgin, Charlton-on-Otmoor, Oxfordshire
first Sunday in May	'Cowslip Sunday' and Blessing the Stream Lambley, Nottinghamshire
	Service and Cheese-Rolling St John the Baptist Church, Randwick, Gloucestershire.
Rogation Monday	Bidding for Grazing Rights Wishford Magna, Wiltshire
	The Wilkes Walk Leighton Buzzard, Bedfordshire.
Rogationtide	Blessing the Waters Mudeford, Hampshire
a Monday in May	Blessing of Fishing Boats North Shields and Cullercoats, Tyneside
12 May	Florence Nightingale memorial service Westminster Abbey
	May Garland Ceremony (formerly Blessing of the Fishing Boats) War Memorial, Abbotsbury, Dorset
26 May	Samuel Pepys' Day St Olave's Church, Hart Street, London
29 May	Oak Apple Day Wishford Magna, Wiltshire; Castleton, Derbyshire.
last Sunday in May	Blessing of the Fleet Brixham, Devon
Ascension Eve	Interdenominational Blessing of the Sea Lifeboat Station, Hastings, Sussex
eve of Ascension Day	Penny Hedge Ceremony Whitby, North Yorkshire

Ascension Day	Election of Master of Worshipful Company of Parish Clerks A City of London Livery Hall
	Beating the Bounds various parishes, annually; All-Hallows-by-the-Tower, London (tri-annually)
	Blessing of the Boats Whitby, Yorkshire
	Well-Dressing Tissington and other locations, Derbyshire
	Singing Praetorius's Ascension Day Carol St John's College Chapel Tower, Cambridge
a Sunday in May	Distribution of Oranges St Mary's Church, Sileby, Leicestershire.
a Monday in May	Blessing of the Boats North Shields and Cullercoats, Tyneside
a date late May	Well-dressing Wirksworth, Derbyshire

June

first Tuesday in June	The Bubble Sermon St Martin's-within-Ludgate, London
first Thursday in June	Ladies' Day Walk and Service Neston, Cheshire
Whitsunday/Pentecost	Open-air services Various parishes
Whitsunday or a day in Whitsun	Whit Walks Manchester, Salford, Lancashire and other locations
	Open-air Pentecost Services Various village greens
	Rush Sunday St Mary Redcliffe, Bristol
	St Briavel's Bread and Cheese Dole St Mary's Church, St Briavels, Herefordshire
Whit Tuesday	Dicing for Bibles ceremony All Saints' Church, St Ives, Cambridgeshire

17 June	St Nectan's Day Service and Foxglove Procession St Nectan's Church, Hartland, Devon
Thursday after Trinity Sunday	Corpus Christi Processions Various churches
	Corpus Christi Carpet of Flowers Arundel Cathedral, Sussex
18 June	Pilgrimage and Re-enactment of the Execution of St Alban St Alban's Cathedral, Hertfordshire
22 June	St Wilfrid Pilgrimage Ripon Cathedral, Yorkshire
on or near 24 June	Well-dressing Youlgrave, Derbyshire
nearest Sunday after 29 June	Clypping the Church St Peter's Church, Edgmond, Shropshire
29 June (unless Sunday, then 28 June)	Rushbearing Ceremony St Columba's Church, Warcop, Cumbria and other locations
Sunday nearest 29 June	St Peter's Day – Blessing the Fisheries Folkestone, Kent
	Grass-strewing Wingrave, Buckinghamshire
first Sunday after 29 June	The Rush Sermon St Giles, Farnborough, Kent.
	Hay-strewing St Peter & St Paul, Langham, Rutland
second Sunday after St Peter's day (29 June)	Clypping the Church St Peter's Tankersley, Yorkshire
variable date in June	The Knollys Rose Ceremony All-Hallows-by-the Tower, City of London
a week in late June or early July	Pilgrimage to Hailes Abbey Hailes, Gloucestershire

July

first Saturday in July	Bradwell Pilgrimage St Cedds Chapel, Bradwell, Essex

	Rushbearing Ceremony St Theobald's Church, Great Musgrave
second Saturday in July	Tewkesbury Battle re-enactment and Service of Compline Tewkesbury Abbey
first Sunday in July	Alport Love Feast Alport Castles, Derbyshire
25 July	St James' Day Blessing of the Waters Whitby, Kent
Saturday nearest 26 July	Rushbearing ceremony Ambleside, Cumbria

August

Saturday before first Monday in August	St Wilfrid Parade and Service Ripon Cathedral, Yorkshire
first Sunday in August	Blessing of the Norfolk Broads St Benet's Hulme Abbey, Horning, Norfolk.
Saturday nearest 12 August	Rushbearing Ceremony Grasmere, Cumbria
	Mary Gibson Memorial Service (the tomb inspection no longer occurs) Sutton, Surrey
first Sunday after 12 August	Rush-strewing and service St Stephen's Church, Forest Chapel, Macclesfield
Wednesday after the second Sunday	Well-blessing Barlow, Derbyshire
last Sunday in August	Plague Sunday Eyam, Derbyshire
24 August	St Bartholomew's Day Service, Childrens Race and Bun Distribution St Bartholomew's Hospital Chapel, Sandwich, Kent
	Blessing of the Mead Gulval,Cornwall

September

first Saturday in September	Blessing of Hops or Hop-Hoodening Day Canterbury Cathedral, Kent.

on or near 8 September	Clypping the Church St Mary's Church, Wirkworth, Derbyshire
first weekend in September	Rushbearing Ceremony Sowerby Bridge, West Yorkshire
19 September or after	Clypping the Church St Mary's Church, Painswick, Gloucestershire
19 September	Patronal Festival Garland Ceremony St Mary the Virgin, Charlton-on-Otmoor
Sunday after 14 September	Pig-Face Day (Holy Cross day) Church of the Holy Cross, Avening, Gloucestershire
third Sunday in September (every second year)	Horseman's Sunday St John's Church, Hyde Park, London
Sunday nearest 29 September	Rushbearing Ceremony St Michael's Church, Urswick, Cumbria
Sunday at end of September	Harvest Festival Various churches
	Costermongers' Harvest Parade St Mary-le-Bow, Cheapside, London
after the harvest	Hanging the Corn Dolly St Faith's Church, Overbury, Hereford and Worcs.
a weekend in September	Church Ale St Mary's Church, Wivenhoe, Essex

October

2 October	Matthew Wall Commemoration (Old Man's Day) St Mary's, Braughing, Bishop's Stortford, Hertfordshire
7 October	Lost in the Dark Peal St Mary's Church, Twyford, Hampshire
from second week in October	Harvest corn dolly display All Saints, Siddington, Cheshire
15 October	Edward the Confessor Pilgrimage Westminster Abbey, London.
16 October	The Lion Sermon St Katherine Kree, City of London

mid-October	Blessing the Fish Harvest St Oswald's Church, Flamborough Head, Yorkshire
a Sunday in October	Blessing of the Nets St Nicholas' Church, Great Yarmouth, Norfolk
a date in October	Pilgrimages to the Tomb of Edward the Confessor Westminster Abbey, London

November

1 November	All Saints' Day Services Various churches
2 November	All Souls' Day Services Various churches
5 November or nearest Sunday	Gunpowder Plot Sermon St Mary-le-Bow, Cheapside, London
second Sunday in November	Remembrance Sunday All churches
11 November	St Martin's Day, Firing of the Fenny-Poppers St Martin, Fenny Stratford, Bletchley, Buckinghamshire
20 November	St Edmund Bun Dance, Southwold, Suffolk
22 November	St Cecilia's Day Service St Paul's Cathedral or Westminster Abbey or Westminster Cathedral
23 November	Orange and Lemons distribution St Clement Danes, Strand, London
first Sunday in Advent	Lighting the Advent wreath Various churches
all Sundays in Advent	Services of Light Various churches

December

first Monday after 1 December	Choosing Day All Saints Church, Brightlingsea, Essex
6 December	Enthronement of Boy Bishop Hereford Cathedral, Berden, Hertfordshire; Boston, Lincolnshire; Par, Cornwall and Edwinstone, Nottinghamshire

second Wednesday in December	Holy Thorn-Cutting ceremony Glastonbury, Somerset
	Plygain Services Various locations
Christmas Eve	Service of Nine Lessons and Carols Kings College Chapel, Cambridge and elsewhere
	Midnight Mass and Blessing of the Crib Various churches
	Ringing the Devil's Knell Dewsbury, Yorkshire
Christmas Day	Choristers Distribution of Red Apples Ripon Cathedral, Yorkshire
31 December	New Year's Eve Watchnight Service Various churches
a date in December (tri-annual)	Candle Auction Parish Hall, Aldermaston, Berkshire

Other customs of variable date

daily	Bread Dole Cartmel Priory, Cumbria
every Wednesday and Saturday evening between Easter and the end of October	Candlelit Procession of our Lady Walsingham, Norfolk
early in July every five years (2013, 2018, etc)	Chester Mystery Plays Chester Cathedral, Cheshire
every 21 years	Candle Auction Chedzoy, Somerset

Bibliography

Addleshaw, G.W.O. and Frederick Etchells, 1948, *The Architectural Setting of Anglican Worship*, Faber and Faber.

Addy, Sidney Oldall, 1895, *Household Tales with other Traditional Remains Collected in the Counties of York, Lincoln, Derby, and Nottingham*, David Nutt.

Addy, Sidney Oldall, 1901, 'Garland day at Castleton', *Folk-Lore* 12 394–428

Addy, Sidney Oldall, 1913, *Church and Manor: A study in English economic history*, George Allen and Co.

Addy, Sidney Oldall, 1933, *Evolution of the English House*, G. Allen and Unwin

Andrew, Edgar, 1886, *Old Church Life in Scotland*, Alexander Gardner.

Andrews, William, 1890a, *Yorkshire in Olden Times*, A. Brown and Sons.

Andrews, William, 1890b, *Curiosities of the Church: Studies of curious customs services and records*, Methuen & Co.

Andrews, William, 1891, *Old Church Lore* William Andrews & Co., The Hull Press.

Andrews, William, 1895, *Curious Church Customs*, William Andrews and Co.

Andrews, William, 1898, *The Church Treasury of History, Custom, Folk-Lore, etc.* William Andrews & Co.

Andrews, William, 1899, *Ecclesiastical Curiosities*, William Andrews & Co.

Andrews, William, 1900, *Old Church Life*, W. Andrews and Co.

Ashley, Leonard R.N., 1988, *Elizabethan Popular Culture*, Bowling Green State University Popular Press.

Ashton, J., 1888, *The Fleet, its River, Prison and Marriages*, Scribner and Welford.

Atkinson, J.C. Revd, 1868, *A Glossary of the Cleveland Dialect: Explanatory, derivative, and critical*, J.R. Smith.

Aubrey, John, 1881, *Remaines of Gentilisme and Judaisme*, Folk-Lore Society.

Baker, Margaret, 1974, *Folklore and Customs of Rural England*, David & Charles.

Baker, Margaret, 1977, *Wedding Customs and Folklore*, David & Charles.

Baker-Jones, Doris, 1977, *The Folklore of Hertfordshire*, B.T. Batsford.

Baring-Gould, Sabine, 1892, *Strange Survivals*, Methuen and Co.

Baring-Gould, Sabine, 1900, *A Book of Dartmoor*, Methuen and Co.

Barlow, F., 1980, 'The King's Evil', *The English Historical Review*, 95/374 January, 3-27.

Barnes, Thomas G., 1959, 'County politics and a Puritan cause célèbre', *Transactions of the Royal Historical Society*, 5s:5, 103-22.

Bede, Venerable, 1907, *Bede's Ecclesiastical History of England,* transl., by A. M. Sellar, George Bell and Sons 1907.

Bennett, Margaret, 1992, *Scottish Customs from the Cradle to the Grave*, Polygon.

Beresford, A.J.B., 1874, *Worship in the Church of England*, John Murray.

Black, Maggie, 1981, 'Food as dole', *History Today*, 31, Issue 5, 59.

Black, Maggie, 1981, 'Saints and soul-caking', *History Today*, 31 Issue 11, 60.

Black, Willam George, 1883, *Folk Medicine*, The Folk-Lore Society.

Blakeborough, Richard, 1898, *Wit, Character, Folklore and Customs of the North Riding of Yorkshire,* H. Frowde.

Bolingbroke, L.G., 1892, 'Pre-Elizabethan plays and players in Norfolk', *Norfolk Archaeology*, 11, 332-351.

Bonham-Carter, S., 1940, 'Notes on birth customs', *Folklore*, 51, 116-122.

The Book of Common Prayer, 2007, Oxford UP.

Brand, John, 1813, *Observations on Popular Antiquities,* 3 Vols, F.C. and J. Rivington.

Bray, A.E., 1838, *Traditions, Legends, Superstitions, and Sketches of Devonshire,* J. Murray.

Brayley, Edward Wedlake, 1850, *A Topographical History of Surrey*, 4 Vols, G. Willis.

Brentnall, Margaret, 1975, *Old Customs and Ceremonies of London,* Batsford.

Brewer, E. Cobham, 1894, *Dictionary of Phrase and Fable,* Cassell.

Brown, Theo, 1961, 'Some examples of Post-Reformation folklore in Devon', *Folklore*, 72, 388-399.

Buchanan, Colin, Trevor Lloyd and Harold Miller (eds), 1980, *Anglican Worship Today*, Collins.

Burne, Charlotte and Georgina Frederica Jackson, 1883, *Shropshire Folk-Lore: A sheaf of gleanings,* Trubner and Co.

Burton, Alfred, 1891, *Rushbearing*, Brook and Chrystal.

Bushaway, Bob, 1982, *By Rite: Custom, Ceremony and Community in England 1700-1880,* Junction Books.

Camp, John, 1988, *In Praise of Bells: The Folklore and Tradition of British Bells,* Robert Hale.

Carrington, F.A., 1859, 'Proceedings of the meetings, November 1848', *Archaeological Journal,* Vol 16, 88.

Carver, Michael, 1987, *Underneath English Towns: Interpreting Urban Archaeology,* Batsford.

Christian, Roy, 1966, *Old English Customs*, Country Life Ltd.

Christie, James, 1893, *Some Account of Parish Clerks: More especially of the ancient fraternity of St Nicholas, now known as the Worshipful Company of Parish Clerks,* Privately printed.

Clark, David, 1982, *Between pulpit and pew: folk religion in a North Yorkshire fishing village,* Cambridge UP.

Clarke, W.K.L. and Charles Harris, 1959, *Liturgy and Worship: A companion to the prayer books of the Anglican communion,* SPCK.

Cocks, Alfred Heneage, 1897, *The Church Bells of Buckinghamshire: their inscriptions, founders, uses and traditions,* Jarrold & Sons.

Collins, Sophie, 2007, *A Sussex Miscellany*, Snake River Press.

Cooke, Dorothy and Pamela McNicol (eds), 1989, *A History of Flower Arranging*, Heinemann Professional Publishing.

Cossins, James, 1877, *Reminiscences of Exeter Fifty Years Since*, William Pollard.

Cote, Wolfred Nelson, 1876, *The Archaeology of Baptism,* Yates and Alexander.

Cowrie, L.W., 1996, *Dictionary of British Social History*, Wordsworth.

Cox, J. Charles, 1913, *Churchwardens' Accounts from the Fourteenth Century to the Close of the Seventeenth Century,* Methuen & Co Ltd.

Crawfurd, Raymond, 1917, 'The blessing of cramp rings' in C. Singer (ed), *Studies in the History and Method of Science*, Clarendon Press.

Cressy, David, 1989, *Bonfire & Bells,* Weidenfeld and Nicolson Ltd.

Cressy, David, 1993, 'Purification, thanksgiving and the churching of women in Post-Reformation England', *Past and Present,* 141(10) 106–46 .

Cressy, David, 1997, *Birth, Marriage & Death: Ritual, religion, and the life-cycle in Tudor and Stuart England,* Oxford UP.

Crooke, W., 1909, 'Burial of Suicides at Cross-Roads' *Folklore*, 20, 88-89.

Cutts, Edward L., 1898, *Parish priests and their people,* E & J. B. Young and Co.

Davies, Jonathan Cerredig, 1911, *Folklore of West and Mid-Wales*, printed at the 'Welsh Gazette' offices.

Dawson, Warren R., 1932, 'A Norfolk vicar's charm against ague', *Norfolk Archaeology,*Vol 24, 233-238.

Davies, Owen, 1997, 'Methodism, the clergy and the popular belief in witchcraft and magic', *History: Journal of the Historical Association*, Volume 82, April, Issue 266, 197–391.

Day, Brian, 1999, *A Chronicle of Folk Customs: A day to day guide to folk traditions*, Hamlyn.

Dendy, D.R. 1959, *The Use of Lights in Christian Worship*, Alcuin Club Collections No. 41, SPCK.

Denham, Michael Aislabie, 1895, *The Denham tracts: A collection of folklore*, The Folklore Society.

Ditchfield, P.H., 1896, *Old English Customs extant at the Present Time,* G. Redway.

Ditchfield, P. H., 1907, *The Parish Clerk*, Methen & Co.

Dryden, Alice, 1911, *Memorials of Old Leicestershire,* G. Allen & Sons.

Drury, Susan, 1994, 'Funeral plants and flowers in England: Some examples', *Folklore*, 105, 101-103.

Duffy, Eamon, 1992, *The Stripping of the Altars: Traditional religion in England 1400–1580*, Yale UP.

Dyer, T.F. Thiselton, 1891, *Church Lore Gleanings*, A.D. Innes & Co.

Dyer, T.F. Thiselton, 1898, *Old English Social Life as told by Parish Registers*, E. Stock.

Dyer, T.F. Thiselton, 1900*, British Popular Customs Present and Past,* George Bell & Sons.

Dymond, David, 1998, 'Swarming the church', *Folklore*, 109, 110-111.

Eaton, Tim, 2001, *Plundering the Past: Roman Stonework in Medieval Britain,* Tempus.

Edwards, H., 1842, *A Collection of Old English Customs and Curious Bequests and Charities,* J. Bower.

Entwhistle, Dorothy, 2012, 'The Whit Walks of Hyde: Glorious spectacle, religious witness and celebration of a custom', *Journal of Religious History,* Vol 36, Issue 2, 204–33.

Ettlinger, Ellen, 1962, 'Folklore in Oxfordshire churches', *Folklore,* 73, 160-177.

Ettlinger, Ellen, 1967, 'Folklore in Buckinghamshire churches', *Folklore,* 78, 275–292.

Fanning, William, 1907, 'Baptism', in C.G. Herbermann (ed), *The Catholic Encyclopedia,* Robert Appleton Company.

Feasey, Henry John, 1897, *Ancient English Holy Week Ceremonial,* T. Baker.

Finucane, Ronald C., 1977, *Miracles and Pilgrims: Popular Beliefs in Medieval England,* Rowman and Littlefield.

French, Richard Valpey, 1884, *Nineteen Centuries of Drink in England: A History,* National Temperance Publication Depot.

Forby, Robert, 1830, *The Vocabulary of East Anglia,* J.B. Nichols and Sons.

Gasquet, Abbot, 1906, *Parish Life in Medieval England,* The Antiquary's Books.

Gennep, A. van, 1960, *The rites of passage,* Routledge and Kegan Paul.

Gerish, W. B., 1911, *Folk-lore of Hertfordshire,* Bishop's Stortford.

Gilchrist, James, 1967, *Anglican Church Plate,* Connoisseur and Michael Joseph.

Gloucestershire Notes and Queries

Gomme, George Laurence, 1883, *Folk-lore Relics of Early Village Life,* Elliot Stock.

Gomme, George Laurence, 1892, *Ethnology in Folklore,* Kegan Paul, Trench, Trübner.

Good, Jabez, 1906, *A Glossary or Collection of Words, Phrases, Place Names, Superstitions, &c., Current in East Lincolnshire,* H. Pulford.

Goody, Jack, 1993, *The Culture of Flowers,* Cambridge UP.

Greenwell, Paul, 2012, Email 03 May, <canonpaul@riponcathedral.org.uk.>

Grose, Francis, 1787, *Antiquities of England and Wales,* Hooper & Wigstead.

Gurevich, Aron, 1988, *Medieval popular culture: Problems of belief and perception.* Cambridge Studies in Oral and Literate Culture. Cambridge UP.

Gutch, Mabel, and Mabel Peacock, 1908, *County Folk Lore Vol V, Printed Extracts No VII Examples Of Printed Folk-Lore Concerning Lincolnshire,* Folk-Lore Society.

Hackwood, Frederick W., 1909, *Inns, Ales and Drinking Customs of Old England,* T. Fisher Unwin.

Hardman, J.W., 1890, *Our Prayer Book in History, Literature and Church Lore,* Skeffington & Son.

Hare, Augustus, J.C., 1872, *Memorials of a quiet life,* Strahan & Co.

Harland, J. and T.T. Wilkinson, 1873, *Lancashire Legends, Traditions, Pageants, Sports, Etc.,* G. Routledge.

Harte, Jeremy, 2008, *English Holy Wells: A Sourcebook,* Heart of Albion.

Hartland, M.E., 1913, 'Breconshire village folklore', *Folklore,* 24, 505-517.

Hartland, E. Sidney, 1893-4, 'The Whitsunday rite at St Briavels', *Transactions of the Bristol and Gloucestershire Archaeological Society,* Vol 18, 82-93.

Hawkins, D. 1990, 'Death and the new London cemeteries of 1348', *Antiquity,* 64, 637-42.

Hearne, Thomas, 1857, *Reliquiae Hearnianae: The remains of Thomas Hearne ... Being extracts from his ms. diaries,* P. Bliss.

Henderson, William, 1879, *Folklore of the Northern Counties of England and the Borders,* W. Satchell.

Heslop, Richard Oliver, 1892, *Northumberland Words: A glossary of words used in the County of Northumberland and on the Tyneside,* K. Paul, Trench, Trübner & Co.

Hole, Christina, 1942, *English Custom and Usage,* Batsford, Ltd.

Hole, Christina, 1953, *The English Housewife in the Seventeenth Century,* Chatto & Windus.

Hole, Christina, 1978, *A Dictionary of British Folk Customs,* Paladin.

Hone, W. 1838, *The Yearbook of Daily Recreation and Information,* Thomas Tegg & Son.

Houlebrooke, Ralph A., 1995, *The English Family 1450-1700,* Longman.

Hunt, Cecil, 1954, *British Customs and Ceremonies: When, Where and Why,* Ernest Benn Ltd.

Hutton, Ronald, 1994, *The Rise and Fall of Merry England,* Oxford UP.

Hutton, Ronald, 1995, 'The English Reformation and the evidence of folklore', *Past and Present,* No. 148, August, 89-116.

Hutton, Ronald, 1996, *The Stations of the Sun: A history of the ritual year in Britain,* Oxford UP.

Hutton, Ronald, 2011, 'How pagan were medieval English peasants?', *Folklore,* 122, 235-249.

Ingram, Tom, 1954, *Bells in England,* Frederick Muller Ltd.

Jeafferson, John C., 1870, *A Book about the Clergy,* Vols. 1 and 2, Hurst and Blackett.

Jeffrey, Percy Shaw, 1923, *Whitby Lore and Legend,* Horne.

Jewitt, L., 1853, 'On ancient customs and sports in the county of Notts', *Journal British Archaeological Association,* 8, 229-240.

Jolly, Karen, 1996, *Popular Religion in Late Saxon England,* University of North Carolina Press.

Jones, William, 1877, *Finger-ring lore: Historical, legendary and anecdotal,* Chatto & Windus.

Jupp, Peter C., and Clare Gittings, 1999, *Death in England: An illustrated history,* Manchester UP.

Kent, Sylvia, 2005, *Folklore of Essex,* Tempus Publishing Ltd.

Kightly, Charles, 1986, *The Customs and Ceremonies of Britain: An encyclopaedia of living traditions,* Thames & Hudson.

Kilvert, Francis, 1977, *Kilvert's Diary 1870-1879,* Ed. William Plomer, Penguin.

King, Pamela J., 1992, 'The Virgins' Crown'. Downloaded October 2010 from www.little-ann.co.uk/church/virgins.htm

Kittredge, George Lyman, 1929, *Witchcraft in Old and New England,* Harvard UP.

Lamborn, E.A. Greening, 1912, *The Story of Architecture in Oxford Stone,* Clarendon Press.

Larner, Christina, 1984, *Witchcraft and Religion: The politics of popular belief,* Basil Blackwell Ltd.

Latham, Charlotte, 1878, 'Some West Sussex superstitions lingering in 1868', *The Folk-Lore Record,* 1, 1-67.

Lawrence, Robert Means, 1898, *The Magic of the Horseshoe, with other Folk-lore Notes*, Houghton, Mifflin & Co.

Law, L.A., 1900, 'Death and burial customs in Wiltshire', *Folklore* 11, 344-347.

Legg, Edward, 2001, *The Fenny Poppers, St Martin's Day Celebrations Fenny Stratford, Bucks*, Word Merchant.

Legg, J. Wickham (Ed.), 1903, *The Clerks Book of 1549*, Henry Bradshaw Society

Legg, J. Wickham, 1921, *English Church life from the Restoration to the Tractarian Movement* , Longmanns, Green & Co.

Leather, E.M., 1912, *The Folklore of Herefordshire,* Jakeman & Carver.

Lister, M., email 30 August <twft@dsl.pipex.com>.

Lloyd, Bertram, 1945, 'Notes on Pembrokeshire folk-lore, superstitions, dialect words, etc', *Folklore*, 56, 307-320.

Lovett, Edward, 1925, *Magic in Modern London*, Croydon: Croydon Advertiser.

Mackenzie, Neil, 1987, 'Boy into Bishop', *History Today*, 37, 10-16.

Malkin, Benjamin Heath, 1804, *The Scenery, Antiquities and Biography of South Wales,* Longman and Rees.

Marks, R., 2004, *Image and Devotion in Late Medieval England*, Stroud.

Markus, R.A., 1990, *The End of Ancient Christianity*, Cambridge UP.

Mikkelson, Barbara, 'Smock Weddings'. Downloaded October 2011 from www.snopes.com/weddings/customs/smock.asp

Miles, Clement, A., 1912, *Christmas in Ritual and Tradition, Christian and Pagan*, T. Fisher Unwin.

Monger, George, 2004, *Marriage Customs of the World: From henna to honeymoons*, ABC-CLIO

Neale, John Mason, 1846, *A Few Words to Parish Clerks and Sextons of Country Parishes*, The Camden Society, Third Edition.

Nelson, Eric, 2002, *The Jesuit Legend: Superstition and mythmaking* in Parish, in H. Parish and W.G. Naphy, (Eds.) *Religion and Superstition in Reformation Europe*, Manchester UP.

Newall, Victoria, 1985, 'Folklore and cremation', *Folklore,* 96, 139-155.

Nicholson, John, 1890, *Folklore of East Yorkshire*, Simpkin, Marshall. Hamilton, Kent & Co.

Noake, John, 1868, *Noake's Guide to Worcestershire*, Longman and Co.

North, Thomas, 1876, *The Church Bells of Leicestershire,* S. Clarke.

North, Thomas, 1883, *The Church Bells of Bedfordshire*, E. Stock.

Obelkevich, James, 1976, *Religion and Rural Society: South Lindsey 1825-1875,* Clarendon Press.

O'Connor, Anne, 2005, *The Blessed and the Damned: Sinful women and unbaptised children in folklore,* Peter Lang.

Opie, Iona and Moira Tatem (eds), 1989, *Dictionary of Superstitions*, Oxford UP.

Owen, Trefor, 1987, *Welsh Folk Customs*, Gomer.

Palmer, Roy, 1976, *Folklore of Warwickshire*, Batsford.

Palmer, Roy, 1985, *The Folklore of Leicestershire and Rutland,* Sycamore Press.

Parish, W.D., 1875, *A Dictionary of the Sussex Dialect*, Farncombe & Co.

Partridge, J.B., 1912, 'The game of "Thread the Needle" and custom of church clipping', *Folklore*, 23, 196-203.

Peacock, Mabel, 1927, *The Folklore and Legends of Lincolnshire,* England, s.n.

Pollard, Alfred W. 1927, *English Miracle Plays, Moralities and Interludes: Specimens of the pre-Elizabethan Drama,* The Clarendon Press.

Porter, Enid, 1969, *Cambridgeshire Customs and Folklore,* Routledge & Kegan Paul.

Postles, David, 2007, 'Micro-spaces: church porches in pre-modern England', *Journal of Historical Geography,* Volume 33, Issue 4, October, 749–69.

Puckle, Bertram S., 1926, *Funeral Customs,* reprinted 2008, Forgotten Books.

Purcell, William, 1981, *Pilgrim's England,* Longman Group Ltd.

Radford, Edwin and Mona A. Radford, 1949, *Encyclopedia of Superstitions,* The Philosophical Library.

Radford Edwin and Mona A. Radford, 1961, (Ed. and revised by Christina Hole) *Encyclopaedia of Superstitions,* Hutchinson.

Rawnsley, E.F., 1953, *The Rushbearing in Grasmere and Ambleside,* Titus Wilson.

Rock, Daniel, 1853, *The Church of Our Fathers,* Vols. 1-3, C. Dolman.

Roberts, George, 1856, *The Social History of the people of the Southern Counties,* Longman, Brown, Green, Longmans and Roberts.

Robinson, Francis Kildale, 1855, *A Glossary of Yorkshire Words and Phrases, Collected in Whitby and the Neighbourhood,* J.R. Smith.

Roud, Steve, 2006, *The English Year,* Penguin Books.

Rudkin, Ethel H., 1933, 'Lincolnshire folklore', *Folklore,* 44, 279-295.

Rushton, Peter, 1980, 'A note on the survival of popular Christian magic', *Folklore,* 91, 115-118

Savory, Arthur H., 1920, *Grain and Chaff from an English Manor,* B. Blackwell.

Seaburg, Carl, 2004, *Celebrating Christmas: An Anthology,* iUniverse.

Sheingorn, Pamela, 1987, *The Easter sepulchre in England,* Medieval Institute Publications.

Shuel, Brian, 1985, *The National Trust Guide to the Traditional Customs of Britain,* Webb and Bower.

Simpson, Jacqueline, 1976, *The Folklore of the Welsh Border,* Batsford.

Simpson, Jacqueline and Steve Roud, 2000, *A Dictionary of English Folklore,* Oxford UP.

Smith, Alan, 1971, *The Established Church and Popular Religion 1750-1850,* Longman

Smolden, William L., 1946, 'The Easter sepulchre music-drama', *Music & Letters,* Vol. 27, No. 1 (Jan), 1-17.

Spicer, Dorothy Gladys, 1954, *Yearbook of English Festivals,* H.W. Wilson Co.

Stackhouse, Thomas, 1737, *The miseries and great hardships of the inferior clergy in and about London,* J. Roberts.

Stockdale, James, 1872, *Annales Caermoelenses or Annals of Cartmel,* Simpkin, Marshall and Co.

Suggett, Richard, 1996, 'Festivals and social structure in early modern Wales', *Past and Present,* 152 (1), 79–112.

Tarlow, Sarah, 2011, *Ritual, Belief and the Dead in Early Modern Britain and Ireland,* Cambridge UP.

Tate, W.E., 1946, *The Parish Chest,* Cambridge UP.

Thomas, Keith, 1997, *Religion and the Decline of Magic,* Weidenfield and Nicholson.

Tongue, R. L., 1958, 'Odds and ends of Somerset folklore', *Folklore,* 69, 43-45.

Tongue, R. L., 1962, 'The open grave', *Folklore*, 73, 106-108.

Trevelyan, Marie, 1909, *Folklore and Folk Stories of Wales*, E. Stock.

Trubshaw, R.N., 1990, 'Hallaton Hare-Pie Scramble and Bottle-Kicking', *Northern Earth Mysteries,* 41 (January), 17–20.

Trubshaw, R.N. 2002, *Explore Folklore*, Explore Books.

Turton, Robert B., 1909, 'The service of Horngarth', *Yorkshire Archaeological Journal* 20, 51-67.

Tyack, George S., 1899, *Lore and Legend of the English Church*, William Andrews and Co.

Unwin, Philip, 1978, *The Stationers' Company 1918-1977: A livery company in the modern world,* Ernest Benn.

Urlin, Ethel, L., 1915, *Festivals, Holy Days and Saints Days*, Simpkin, Marshall, Hamilton, Kent & Co.

Vaux, J. Edward, 1894, *Church Folklore*, G. Farran.

Vickery, Roy, 1995, *A Dictionary of Plant Lore*, Oxford UP.

Walcott, Mackenzie, 1872, *The Customs and Traditions of Cathedrals,* Longmans, Green and Co.

Walters, H.B., 1912, *Church Bells of England*, Oxford UP.

Warner, Marina, 1992, 'Speaking with double tongue: mother goose and the old wives' tale', in R. Porter (Ed.), *Myths of the English,* Polity Press.

Watkins, Carl, 2004, '"Folklore" and "Popular Religion" in Britain during the Middle Ages', *Folklore,* 115, 140--50.

Wilkinson, Jeffrey, 2010, 'Time future contained in time past', *Church Times,* July 16, 32–33.

Williams, E. Carleton, 1949, 'The Aldermaston candle auction', *Berkshire Archaeological Journal,* 51, 35–40.

Williamson, George, C., 1923, *Curious Survivals: Habits and customs of the past that still live in the present,* H. Jenkins.

Wilson, Stephen, 2004, *The Magical Universe: Everyday ritual and magic in pre-modern Europe,* Hambledon and London.

Witcutt, W.P., 1941, 'Notes on Staffordshire Folklore', *Folklore* 52, 236-237.

Wolesley, Viscountess, 1921, *The Countryman's log-book*, P. L. Warner & J. Cape.

Wright, Arthur Robinson, 1928, *English Folklore,* Ernest Benn Ltd.

Wright, A.W. and Lones, T.E. (eds), 1940, *British Calendar Customs*, Folklore Society, 3 Vols.

Wright, Elizabeth Mary, 1913, *Rustic Speech and Folk-Lore*, Oxford UP.

Yonge, Charlotte M., 1892, *An old woman's outlook in a Hampshire village,* Macmillan and Co.

Young, K. 1933, *The Drama of the Medieval Church*, 2 Vols, Clarendon Press.

Index

EXPLORE GREEN MEN

Revised and expanded second edition

Mercia MacDermott

with photographs by Ruth Wylie

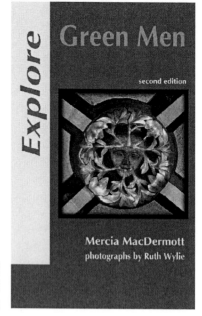

Explore Green Men is the first detailed study of the history of this motif for 25 years. Dr MacDermott's research follows the Green Man back from the previous earliest known examples into its hitherto unrecognised origins in India about 2,300 years ago.

The book starts by discussing the 'paganisation' of Green Men in recent decades, then follows backwards through the Victorian Gothic Revival, Baroque, Rococco and Italianate revivals, to their heyday in the Gothic and the supposed origins in the Romanesque. As part of this discussion there is background information on the cultural changes that affected how Green Men were regarded. The author also discusses the comparisons that have been made with Cernunnus, Robin Hood, Jack-in-the-Green, woodwoses, Baphomet, Al Khidr and Bulgarian peperuda. She also investigates which pagan god Green Men supposedly represent.

The second edition contains a summary of independent confirmation of the links with Asia together with nine more illustrations.

Explore Green Men is illustrated with 118 photographs and drawings, mostly of Green Men who have never before showed their faces in books.

This book will appeal to all with an interest in Green Men and to art historians looking for a reliable study of this fascinating decorative motif.

Published by Explore Books, an imprint of Heart of Albion Press. ISBN 978 1 872883 946. 2006. demy 8vo (215 x 138 mm), 212 + x pages, 109 b&w photographs, 8 line drawings, 1 map, paperback, **£12.95**

EXPLORE FOLKLORE

Bob Trubshaw

'A howling success, which plugs a big and obvious gap'

Professor Ronald Hutton

"Highly Recommended" by the Folklore Society's Katharine Briggs Folklore Award 2003

There have been fascinating developments in the study of folklore in the last twenty-or-so years, but few books about British folklore and folk customs reflect these exciting new approaches. As a result there is a huge gap between scholarly approaches to folklore studies and 'popular beliefs' about the character and history of British folklore. Explore Folklore is the first book to bridge that gap, and to show how much 'folklore' there is in modern day Britain.

Explore Folklore shows there is much more to folklore than morris dancing and fifty-something folksingers! The rituals of 'what we do on our holidays', funerals, stag nights and 'lingerie parties' are all full of 'unselfconsious' folk customs. Indeed, folklore is something that is integral to all our lives – it is so intrinsic we do not think of it as being 'folklore'.

The implicit ideas underlying folk lore and customs are also explored. There might appear to be little in common between people who touch wood for luck (a 'tradition' invented in the last 200 years) and legends about people who believe they have been abducted and subjected to intimate body examinations by aliens. Yet, in their varying ways, these and other 'folk beliefs' reflect the wide spectrum of belief and disbelief in what is easily dismissed as 'superstition'.

Explore Folklore provides a lively introduction to the study of most genres of British folklore, presenting the more contentious and profound ideas in a readily accessible manner.

Published by Explore Books, an imprint of Heart of Albion Press. ISBN 978 1872 883 601. 2002. demy 8vo (215 x 138 mm), 196 xii pages, 4 b&w photos, 4 line drawings, paperback, **£12.95**

HUNKY PUNKS

A study in Somerset stone carving

Peter Poyntz Wright

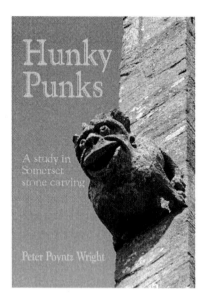

High up on the famous church towers of Somerset, almost lost to the eye except for their silhouettes, are an amazing series of grotesque stone figures. Carved in the fifteenth and sixteenth centuries, to ornament corners and break up straight sections of masonry, these figures are known in some rural areas at hunky punks.

This book combines a fascinating historical and architectural study with a stunning collection of photographs. Peter Poyntz-Wright's research provides the first thorough account of the hunky punks and gives us a direct insight into the medieval mind. He examines the techniques and influences of the medieval masons, and considers methods of attachment and the effects of weathering.

The author has recorded a host of hitherto unknown and inaccessible medieval carvings the first time – and possibly for the last. They include such creatures as dragons, griffins, hounds, stags, heraldic creatures, a basilisk, the devil, a woman in childhood, and many others. However many of the hunk punks are suffering seriously from the effects of wearing, and some, without costly restoration, may not survive for many more years.

ISBN 978 1872 883 755. 2004. A5 (210 x 148 mm), 156 + x pages, 76 black and white photographs; 3 line drawings, paperback. (new edition with revised photographs, **£9.95**

A BESTIARY OF BRASS

Peter Heseltine

'This is a beautifully
produced volume...'
Paul Cockerham
*Journal of Church
Monuments*

From antelopes to wyverns, with over fifty
species in between, *A Bestiary of Brass*
looks the animals, birds, insects, fish – even
shellfish – which have been depicted on
medieval memorial brasses in Britain. Some are native, others – such as
elephants and panthers – were exotic, while dragons and unicorns were as
mythical then as they are today.

At the time they were engraved these creatures evoked a wide range of
folklore and legends. This rich symbolism is brought to life by the author. But
enigmas remain – why would anyone want to be associated with a fox when
they were more noted for cunning and slyness, or a hedgehog, or even a
whelk? We also find out about the lives of the people commemorated and
share the author's detailed knowledge of their heraldic emblems. Practical
advice is provided to help make brass rubbings and to learn more about
these memorials.

The illustrations show a wide range of the memorials, with detailed views of
the creatures they incorporate. *A Bestiary of Brass* will appeal to anyone
interested in folklore, art and medieval history. Above all, these masterpieces
of craftsmanship reveal that our deep fascination with animals was shared by
our ancestors many hundreds of years ago.

ISBN 978 1872 883 908. 2006. Demy 8vo (215 x 138 mm), 227 + x pages,
308 b&w drawings and photographs, paperback., **£12.95**

ENGLISH HOLY WELLS:

A sourcebook

Jeremy Harte

'It is difficult to exaggerate
the service Jeremy Harte has
done the study of hydrolatry
in English Holy Wells.'

James Rattue author of The
Living Stream

What happens if you track down the earliest known reference to every holy well in England? The vivid traditions of these sites, many of them hitherto unknown, cast a new light on whether holy wells were taken over from pagan precursors, and what the Reformation meant for sacred landscapes. Colourful tales of saints, sprites and charlatans reveal the lively side of medieval popular religion.

With this book the study of English holy wells moves out of the realms of romanticism and myth-making into the light of history. Jeremy Harte draws on maps, miracles, legends and landscapes to present his detailed discussions in a readable and often witty manner.

Jeremy Harte is a folklorist with a particular interest in sacred places and supernatural encounters. His other books include *Explore Fairy Traditions, Cuckoo Pounds and Singing Barrows, The Green Man, Research in Geomancy* and *Alternative Approaches to Folklore*. He is curator of Bourne Hall Museum in Surrey.

English Holy Wells comprises three volumes. Volume One is supplied with a CD-ROM of Volumes Two and Three to make the complete work available at an affordable price.

Volume One (includes CD-ROM of Volumes Two and Three):
ISBN 978-1-905646-10-4, 245 x 175 mm, 168 + xvi pages, 24 b&w line drawings, paperback, 2008. **£14.95**

HOLY WELLS IN BRITAIN

A guide

Janet Bord

The secrets of Britain's
most evocative sacred sites

Holy wells were once widespread throughout Britain. They were often dedicated to local saints and were important features in the medieval sacred landscape. Over many centuries, pilgrims sought the healing powers of their waters, and many left votive offerings in the form of bent pins, coins and rags.

Interest in this aspect of our sacred heritage has been growing since the publication of Janet Bord's first book on holy wells over twenty years ago. Many holy wells have now been restored, and the modern visitor may still experience a quiet communion with the spirit of the place, and come away spiritually uplifted.

For this book Janet Bord has sought out three hundred of the surviving holy wells of England, Wales and Scotland that are most rewarding to visit, and she recounts their histories and traditions in the light of current historical research.

Holy Wells in Britain is the first guidebook to British holy wells to draw upon the extensive research of recent decades. Up-to-date practical information for visitors is also provided to inspire readers to seek out these evocative sacred sites for themselves.

ISBN 978-1-905646-09-8 April 2008. 245 x 175 mm, 226 + xii pages, 179 b&w photos, 5 line drawings, paperback. **£14.95**

Heart of Albion

Publishing folklore, mythology and
local history since 1989

Further details of all Heart of Albion titles online at
www.hoap.co.uk

All titles available direct from Heart of Albion Press.

Heart of Albion Press

113 High Street, Avebury
Marlborough, SN8 1RF

Phone: 01672 539077
email: albion@indigogroup.co.uk
Web site: www.hoap.co.uk